FROM PIONEER TO NOMAD

ESSAYS ON ITALIAN NORTH AMERICAN WRITING

ESSAY SERIES 48

Guernica Editions Inc. acknowledges the support of
The Canada Council for the Arts.
Guernica Editions Inc. acknowledges the support of
the Ontario Arts Council.
Guernica Editions Inc. acknowledges the financial support of
the Government of Canada through the Book Publishing Industry
Development Program (BPIDP).

LEONARDO BUONOMO

FROM PIONEER TO NOMAD

ESSAYS ON ITALIAN NORTH AMERICAN WRITING

GUERNICA

TORONTO · BUFFALO · CHICAGO · LANCASTER (U.K.)

2003

Copyright © 2003, by Leonardo Buonomo and Guernica Editions Inc.
All rights reserved. The use of any part of this publication, reproduced, transmitted in any form or by any means, electronic, mechanical, photocopying, recording or otherwise stored in a retrieval system, without the prior consent of the publisher is an infringement of the copyright law.

Antonio D'Alfonso, editor
Guernica Editions Inc.
P.O. Box 117, Station P, Toronto (ON), Canada M5S 2S6
2250 Military Road, Tonawanda, N.Y. 14150-6000 U.S.A.

Distributors:
University of Toronto Press Distribution,
Gazelle Book Services, Falcon House, Queen Square,
Lancaster LA1 1RN U.K.

First edition.
Printed in Canada.

Legal Deposit – First Quarter
National Library of Canada
Library of Congress Catalog Card Number: 2003101161

National Library of Canada Cataloguing in Publication
Buonomo, Leonardo
From pioneer to nomad :
essays on Italian North American writing / Leonardo Buonomo.
(Essay series ; 48)
ISBN 1-55071-166-0
1. American literature – Italian American authors – History and criticism.
2. Verdicchio, Pasquale, 1954- – Criticism and interpretation.
I. Title. II. Series: Essay series (Toronto, Ont.) 48
PS153.I8B86 2002   810.9'851   C2002-905354-4

CONTENTS

Acknowledgments 6

Foreword 9

Early Narratives by Italian Americans:
Luigi Palma di Cesnola's "Ten Months in Libby Prison" . . 13

"Ten Months in Libby Prison" 23

Monaca o strega?:
The Catholic Missionary as Outsider in Sister Blandina
Segale's *At the End of the Santa Fe Trail* 37

A "Lost Soul" in America:
Emanuel Carnevali's Autobiography 49

The Italian American Man's Burden:
Masculinity in John Fante and Jerre Mangione 61

A Dissenter's Return:
John Fante's Novel for the 1980s 74

"In the Name of the Farther":
The Poetry of Pasquale Verdicchio 85

Notes 95

Works Cited 98

ACKNOWLEDGMENTS

I wish to express my gratitude to the friends and colleagues who helped me in different ways during the preparation of this work: Gabrielle Barfoot, William Boelhower, Nicholas Carter, Antonio D'Alfonso, Giordano De Biasio, Claire Fennell, and Pasquale Verdicchio. I am also grateful to the growing number of critics and scholars of Italian American writing whose work has been a powerful source of inspiration and guidance for my own investigations. A shorter version of the essay on Cesnola appeared in *Red Badges of Courage: Wars and Conflicts in American Culture*, edited by Biancamaria Pisapia, Ugo Rubeo, and Anna Scacchi (Rome: Bulzoni, 1999). "*Monaca o Strega?*" was originally published, in a slightly different form, in *Voices in Italian Americana* 2 (1993). "A Lost Soul" appeared in *Remembering the Individual, Regional, National Past*, edited by Waldemar Zacharasiewicz (Tübingen: Stauffenburg Verlag, 1999)."In the Name of the Farther" previously appeared in *Adjusting Sites*, edited by William Boelhower and Rocco Pallone (New York: Forum Italicum, 1999).

This book is dedicated
to the memory of
Aldo Buonomo and Mauro Canessa

FOREWORD

The recent publication of *Italoamericana: Storia e letteratura degli italiani negli Stati Uniti 1776-1880*, the first volume of an anthology edited by Francesco Durante, is just the latest sign of the burgeoning interest in Italian American studies. The title of this monumental work inevitably calls to mind the famous 1941 anthology *Americana*, edited by Elio Vittorini, which acknowledged the emergence of an Italian American writer of note, John Fante.[1] An additional link between the two anthologies is the fact that Durante has translated into Italian several of Fante's works and has been instrumental in the rediscovery of this author.

What I would like to emphasize, however, is that with *Italoamericana*, and other publications on Italian American writers that have recently appeared on both sides of the Atlantic,[2] we are well beyond the "discovery" phase. The existence of this branch of North American literature no longer needs to be proven or vindicated. The current efforts of critics and scholars aim at documenting and studying the richness and complexity of Italian American writing rather than simply tracing its evolution. In this sense the dates in the subtitle of Durante's anthology are significant. Not only do they indicate that there were Italian American writers before the mass immigration that began in 1880, but that their appearance coincided with the very birth of the United States. Indeed, one could go even further back in time and take into consideration the Italian contribution to colonial American literature, as represented by the letters and memoirs of early missionaries (such as Father Francesco Eusebio Chini [c.1645-1711]) and explorers (such as Enrico Tonti [1650-1704]).

Though small, the selection of authors analyzed in the following essays represents a wide range of cultural experiences and backgrounds, as well as different phases in the history of Italian American writing. The various regional and social origins of these authors, their different sets of cultural references, find expression in a variety of perspectives and expressions that belie the simplifying and stereotyping images of Italian Americans that still survive in North America. It is the common lot of all ethnic minorities to be denied complexity by the dominant culture, to be reduced to a set of easily recognizable elements, such as physical types, social roles and, most damagingly, pseudo-character-traits. This is why, I believe, one senses in the writers of these groups a special urgency, an eagerness to be heard, to explain who they are. This is certainly true of the writers I concentrate upon in this book. In mid-nineteenth century America the Italian nobleman-turned-immigrant Luigi Palma di Cesnola had to find his place in a society where personal enterprise and merit took precedence over the claims of descent. The Civil War gave him the chance to display his military skills and, more importantly, to play a role in one of his adoptive country's defining rites of passage. As a prisoner of the Confederate Army at Libby Prison, Cesnola himself was severely tested. Deprived of freedom and literally divested of the visible signs of authority and dignity, Cesnola fought a personal battle to defend his worth as a soldier and a human being in the harshest of circumstances. At the same time he did what he could to provide his fellow prisoners with material and moral support and remained throughout his captivity an alert and scrupulous witness to the terrible living conditions at Libby. His indignation at the mistreatment of prisoners, and his need to come to terms with what he had been through, found expression in his powerful memoir "Ten Months in Libby Prison," which this book finally makes available to the modern reader.

It would be difficult to imagine anything more remote from the stereotype of the Italian American woman, solely devoted to home and family, than the portrait Sister Blandina Segale drew of herself in *At the End of the Santa Fe Trail*. As a woman in her early twenties, in 1872, Segale defied her beloved father and left family and friends in Ohio for a distant mining town in Colorado, where she had been assigned by her religious order, the Sisters of Charity. There, and later in New Mexico, she became an active force in the community, a defender of religious freedom, legality and the rights of Native Americans and Hispanics. In the letters she wrote to her sister and fellow missionary Justina, which later became *At the End of the Santa Fe Trail*, the Italian-born Segale assumed the role of spokeswoman for all oppressed minorities. Her memoir eloquently testifies to her critical, lucid outlook on American life, as well as to her wit, courage and compassion (which could embrace even the terror of the Southwest, outlaw Billy the Kid).

Few writers have rendered the excitement, the alienation, and the cultural shock inherent in the immigrant experience as forcefully as Emanuel Carnevali has done in his autobiography. On the surface, Carnevali's relatively brief American adventure might appear the opposite of the classic rags-to-riches immigrant story, and the tragic circumstances of his forced return to Italy (due to the terrible sickness he contracted in America) a cruel reversal of the paradisiacal image of the New World at the beginning of the twentieth century.

The startlingly original works that were the result of his American experience, however, tell a different story. They are the legacy of a man who was able to translate triumphantly his Old World identity into New World terms at the level that is most important for a writer, the level of language.

For second generation Italian Americans such as Jerre Mangione and John Fante a vocation for writing involved not only the difficult process of coming to terms with one's double consciousness, but also a defiance of the traditional idea of masculinity within their families and communities. Dedicating oneself to such a seemingly ephemeral craft could be seen as a transgression, even a betrayal, in a culture in which men were expected to prove themselves through more concrete, more practical activities. In retrospect the enduring appeal of Mangione's and Fante's writings more than vindicates their choice. Indeed, their works have proved no less durable than the many stone structures erected by generations of Italian American craftsmen in the New World, those craftsmen that Fante himself immortalized in some of his finest stories and novels.

Contemporary author Pasquale Verdicchio, to whom the concluding essay of this volume is devoted, perfectly incarnates the on-going evolution of the Italian and American cultural experience. Equally at home in Italian and English (not to mention Neapolitan), Verdicchio is a sophisticated interpreter of the increasingly complex theme of identity in both the Old and the New World. As his poems and essays eloquently demonstrate, Verdicchio has Cesnola's and Segale's combativeness, Carnevali's capacity to appropriate and poetically transform the language of memory and modernity, and Mangione's and Fante's gift for turning his devotion to words into the stuff literature is made of.

EARLY NARRATIVES BY ITALIAN AMERICANS

Luigi Palma di Cesnola's
"Ten Months in Libby Prison" (1865)

The Italians who moved to the United States before the great wave of immigration in the period 1880-1920 came from a variety of social classes and regional backgrounds. They included missionaries, artists, political refugees, and adventurers who, unlike the vast majority of their successors, possessed a good, and sometimes uncommon, level of instruction. Some of them were able to acquire a sufficient competence in the English language to write and even publish in the idiom of their new country. Their letters, memoirs and narratives represent some of the earliest, still largely neglected, documents of the Italian American experience.

Among the texts that, in my view, deserve to be rediscovered is a fascinating Civil War narrative entitled "Ten Months in Libby Prison" which was originally published in the *Bulletin* of the United States Sanitary Commission in 1865. The author is Luigi Palma di Cesnola (1832-1904), a Union cavalry officer who was wounded and taken prisoner by the Confederate army at the battle of Aldie, Virginia, on June 17, 1863. His full name was actually Count Emanuele Pietro Paolo Maria Luigi Palma di Cesnola and he was a native of Rivarolo Canavese, near Turin. Short though it is, Cesnola's report is clearly the work of a man of unusual qualities and character, and has a power of communication that is forceful and eloquent. Cesnola's life story up until, and during, the

Civil War is a remarkable one and in order to fully appreciate his testimony it may be worth outlining briefly a few episodes of his life.

Born in 1832, he studied in Jesuit and military schools and, at the age of fifteen, enlisted in the Royal Army of Piedmont and Sardinia. Those were the dramatic days of the Piedmontese campaign against the Austrian army led by Radetzky, and Cesnola's astonishingly precocious military career in Italy culminated in March of 1849, when he was promoted from corporal to under-lieutenant on the field, at the battle of Novara. He thus became the youngest officer of that army and was also awarded a silver medal for bravery. In 1854 his rapid ascent to the higher levels of military hierarchy was cut short by a scandal, the nature of which remains unknown. What is certain is that it led the young Cesnola to leave Italy and volunteer for the Crimean War. Fighting with the British army he once again distinguished himself for his courage. After the end of that conflict he traveled through Turkey and the Middle East and in 1858 embarked on a journey that was to take him from Constantinople to New York.

The beginning of what might be called Cesnola's "second life"[1] was certainly neither an easy nor a promising one. For some time he was just a penniless aristocrat (doubly negative in prosperous, republican America), who survived by doing translations, selling his music scores, and giving private lessons in Italian and French. Erik Amfitheatrof has aptly described Cesnola's first encounter with American life as "a more genteel but also a heightened version of the immigrant experience" (110), stressing the fact that, unlike most immigrants, the young man from Rivarolo was out of touch both with American society at large and the restricted society of his fellow expatriates. Perhaps because of his particular background or, rather, because of his own haughty consciousness of such a background, Cesnola would not associate with the other Italians then living in New York.

This life of isolation and poverty came to an end in 1861 (shortly after the outbreak of the Civil War) when he married one of his students, Mary Isabel Reid, daughter of Captain C. Reid of the U.S. Navy. In that same year, with the help of his wife, Cesnola set up a private military academy where, within six months, for a fee of $100 (payable in advance), more than seven hundred students were taught the basics of warfare. Having trained such an impressive number of future officers for the Union Army in such a short time – and made a satisfactory profit – Cesnola closed the school and joined the army himself.

Cesnola's career in the Union army was characterized by an odd succession of dazzling successes and ruinous failures. If his intelligence, charisma, and daring, quickly made him a colonel and the commander of as many as five cavalry regiments simultaneously, his independence and arrogance caused him to be placed twice under arrest. On several occasions he won the utmost admiration of his peers, as when, in Virginia, he led a charge unarmed, but at some point he also suffered the disgrace of being dishonorably dismissed from the army on the charge of stealing government property (the dismissal was revoked after a month and Cesnola returned to his regiment, still a colonel but no longer a commander [McFadden 27-50]).

America was a country where a man of Cesnola's resourcefulness could continually reinvent himself – after the war Cesnola became the American Consul to Cyprus, an archaeologist, and the first Director of the Metropolitan Museum of Art – but also where a foreigner was repeatedly called upon to reassure himself and the public of his identity and loyalties. From the evidence of his writings (both public and private) Cesnola appears to have wavered, for quite a while, between viewing himself as a fervent American citizen, even before officially being one (this happened only after his appointment as Consul in 1865), or as the wronged and mistreated alien.[2] Mostly, it seems to me, he thought of himself as an aristocrat, a soldier, a commander, a fighter both in and outside the army. What is especially intriguing about Cesnola's report "Ten Months in Libby Prison" is that, despite its official character[3] (as a contribution to an inquiry into the treatment of war prisoners), it is largely about the formidable threat that life in a detention camp poses to one's identity and self-esteem.

Cesnola's testimony opens with a remarkably direct, terse and yet carefully phrased statement of the facts:

> I entered the service of the United States in October, 1861, and was captured in Virginia the 17th of June, 1863, at the cavalry engagement of Aldie. I was marched, mostly on foot, more than one hundred miles to Staunton, and thence by railroad conveyed to the rebel capital and confined in the Libby prison. (23)

The passive form "I was marched" effectively emphasizes the indignity of the situation, all the more humiliating for a cavalry officer accustomed, as it were, to looking down at life from the saddle of his horse. Also noteworthy is the use, a little later on, of the word "immured," as if the author had thought the previous term "confined" not sufficiently strong, not quite adequate to the task of rendering on paper the experience of the loss of liberty. It is well to point out that Libby prison, a former tobacco warehouse where about twelve hundred Union officers lived in six bare rooms, was considered one of the worst prisons in the Confederacy. Recalling his arrival there, Cesnola comments on the treatment he received from his enemies with a mixture of resentment and contemptuous irony, of offended military pride and aristocratic hauteur.

> [A] rebel sergeant searched me through from head to foot, in the roughest manner possible. He took away from me every little trinket I had . . . and was angry because he could not find any greenbacks on my person. He ordered me to take off my boots for inspection; I answered him that I always had a servant to perform that service for me . . . He asked me what I had done with my money, and if I had any watch. I told him that a chivalric Southron had stolen my watch and money during the march from Middleburg to Staunton. He began to abuse me, using very profane language and denying my veracity. I told him that perhaps the gentleman intended only to borrow those articles from me. (24)

Here Cesnola denounces what he sees as a violation of his person and rank: once in the hands of his enemies he is divested – both literally and symbolically – of everything that identifies him as an officer and a gentleman ("I entered therefore the gates of a Confederate prison stripped of everything except my spurs, which being screwed into the boots could not be removed" [24]). In the first section of his report Cesnola describes what appears to have been a deliberate attempt – on the part of the prison authorities – to reduce the prisoners to the condition of brutes. He complains of having remained "without a book to read, or a sheet of paper to write, for over five months," of having being forced to sleep "on the bare and often damp plank floor, with neither blanket nor overcoat, nor any other covering," using his boots for a pillow, and bitterly concludes that "dogs had certainly better sleeping accommodations in their kennels than I had there" (25). Cut off from the world, dehumanized, Union officers at Libby were also – in relation to the culture of the time – progressively emasculated:

> We were compelled for several months to wash and scrub

the floor, the kitchen, the tables and the sinks ourselves . . . It may have been a mere chance, but it was precisely when the officers were performing such menial services that the Southern ladies would come to have a peep at the Yankees, who certainly were not looking at that moment to their best advantage. (25)

There is an interesting form of dualism in Cesnola. A sincere, unswerving commitment to the cause of the Union, accompanied by a strong feeling of camaraderie with his fellow Yankee officers and soldiers, coexists awkwardly with an unsuppressed sense of aristocratic superiority. In a highly revealing passage, after voicing his admiration for a Union brigadier general who, uncomplainingly and with a "serene countenance," performed his cleaning duties when it was his turn to do so, Cesnola confesses that "such service was revolting to me, and I always found some good-hearted fellow who, for sake of exercise, would perform it in my stead" (25). That Cesnola could not possibly tolerate any situation or act that would seem to demean his dignity is emphatically confirmed by another episode narrated in the final section of the text. Angered by a remark made by Cesnola while talking to a fellow prisoner, an overseer confronts him rudely and "dares" to place a hand on his shoulder. "If a hot iron had touched my skin," Cesnola recalls, "it would not have maddened me more than his insolent touch did." The inescapable impression is that something akin to an unpardonable sacrilege had been perpetrated: "I turned myself toward him, and in a second I had him by the throat with both my hands, down he went on the floor, and I struck him many times as hard as I could on his face, until my rage was satisfied" (35).

Cesnola is at his most humane and compassionate when he recounts what he saw at Belle Isle, the internment camp for 6,000 Union enlisted men. Having been named commissary of distribution on November 10, 1863, he was required to visit

Belle Isle Prison daily in order to supervise the delivery of boxes of clothing and blankets for the prisoners that were sent by the U. S. Sanitary Commission. For all his experience on the battlefields of Europe and North America, Cesnola was genuinely shocked by the spectacle that confronted him at Belle Isle. Recreating that experience on the page he displays uncommon sensitivity and skill in the way he treats a series of graphic images, building up an impressive crescendo of horror and pity:

> I am a soldier by profession since my boyhood; I have been in several wars in Europe; I am familiar with death, and have seen it in all its different aspects, but my heart has never been moved as it was by the condition of those men at Belle Isle. Their frozen feet wrapped in a piece of blanket or an old flannel shirt, in place of the boots which were taken away from them by their captors, those long, pale, hungry faces, with hair and beard uncut for months; a kind of perpetual motion given to their bodies by the millions of vermin that devoured their very flesh; their emaciated forms, telling at first sight how many long and weary, weary months they had been there fighting against death in the form of scurvy, low fevers, diarrhea, congestion of the lungs, etc.; their feeble voices saying, "Oh! Colonel, do give us something to eat, for God's sake," etc. These scenes, I confess, were to me heartrending in the extreme. (30)

In a passage I quoted earlier Cesnola makes a derisive reference to a "chivalric Southron," a "gentleman" who had stolen his watch. This choice of words is representative of the way in which Cesnola portrays his enemies throughout his report. His aim is clearly to disprove, to subvert, the proudly held and widespread view of the South as a land of gallantry and honor, and to expose its people as brutes, vulgarians, and knaves.[4] The fact that Southerners could have the effrontery and presumption to think of themselves as a sort of aristocracy of the New World seemed to this European aristocrat the ultimate provocation. Significantly enough, on the one occasion in which Cesnola speaks favorably of one of his enemies, there is the suggestion that the man in question is not to be considered a "real" Southerner: "Lieutenant Bossieux . . . was well spoken of universally, and I must confess that I found him gentlemanly, humane and generous-hearted. His name, however, shows his foreign origin, though he may have been born in Richmond" (28).

It was Cesnola's overriding concern that Union men of all ranks should constantly demonstrate by their attitude and demeanor, even in the harshest circumstances, that they were vastly superior to their enemies in terms of valor and moral stature. During his term as commissary of distribution at Belle Isle, Cesnola learned that 400 prisoners had been offered parole on condition that they worked making shoes for the Confederate army, and that the same opportunity would soon be given to the rest of the men as well. Although he had been ordered never to talk to the prisoners, Cesnola decided to intervene. As he explains in his narrative, he felt it was his duty "as a U.S. officer" to thwart the Confederate plan and, after summoning "several of the chiefs of squads," he told them "to inform the men that by going at work for the rebels they were breaking their oath toward the U.S. government, and were helping instead of fighting the enemy of their country" (34-35). As a result, when the guards tried to get a second group of laborers, nobody accepted the offer. Cesnola's role in "instigating the mutiny" was soon discovered and this, together with the brawl I mentioned earlier, led to his dismissal from his commissary post (Marinacci 77-78). From then on his imprisonment became once again total and remained so until his release, in March of 1864.

"Ten Months in Libby Prison" contains no overt reference to the author's national origin except, perhaps, for a passing remark in which Cesnola likens his appearance to that of a "Roman gladiator of olden times" (25). Information on Cesnola's background is only provided by a brief biographical sketch that precedes the first-person narrative: here the author is identified as a "Sardinian of noble family." Interestingly enough, this introduction closes with a reference to the fact that, soon after entering Libby Prison, Cesnola, "with some other foreigners," had been offered "better quarters than their fellow officers had, which proposal was indignantly rejected. 'We are U. S. officers,' they said" (23). Given Cesnola's uncertain status in his adoptive country, at the time the narrative was published, and the fact that he was writing for an official organ of the U. S. Federal government, it is understandable that he would feel the need to appear as focused as possible on his role and duty. Together with his exploits on the battlefield, "Ten Months in Libby Prison" would be a powerful statement of his commitment to America. As we have seen, early in the narrative Cesnola singles out the lack of "a sheet of paper to write for over five months" as one of the harshest deprivations he had had to endure. He had been cruelly denied one of the most basic and effective means by which men, in times of crisis, have traditionally managed to preserve their identity and sanity. By giving him the chance to write for the *Bulletin,* after his release from Libby, the U.S. government was in a sense compensating Cesnola for an essential right that had been taken away from him. And the *Bulletin* thus became the "sheet of paper" where the "foreign" war hero could narrate his experiences and, at the same time, make an indirect but very powerful claim about his right to call himself an American citizen.

What also needs to be considered is that Cesnola had emigrated from a country that at the time was still, as it were, "in the making" and whose people did not have (nor would they have for many years) a deeply rooted sense of national identity. My feeling is that Cesnola needed to be more secure of his standing in the United States before he could look back comfortably upon his culture of origin. Significantly enough, in his 1877 book *Cyprus; Its Ancient Cities, Tombs, and Temples*, based on his experiences as consul and amateur archaeologist on that island, Cesnola seems less reticent about his "composite" identity. If, on the one hand, he proudly proclaims himself the "Representative of the American Republic" (42), on the other he recalls with obvious fondness the "pleasant society" of the Italian consul and his wife and the wonderful hospitality he enjoyed at their house (44). In that residence – a synecdoche for Italy – Cesnola could reconnect with his native culture and play at the same time the role of the successful emigrant returning home in triumph.

Perhaps the best example of the extent to which Cesnola had learned to negotiate his dual identity (what Werner Sollors has described as the American culture of consent and the European culture of descent) is to be found in his remarks about his consular and household employees. Cesnola recalls that his first impression of them was unfavorable, because, in his words: "every one as he approached me, instead of taking my proffered hand, would kiss the tips of my fingers, or make pretence of so doing" (43). If the American in him cringed at the excessive deference and servility of his staff, the Italian aristocrat could be relied upon to take over and deal more effectively with strictly hierarchical relationships. In a telling passage Cesnola mentions that he taught Italian to his collaborators and servants and used primarily that language to communicate with them. In the language of his past, Mr. Cesnola could once again (whether by design or not) be Conte Palma di Cesnola.

TEN MONTHS IN LIBBY PRISON

*by Luigi Palma di Cesnola
late Colonel 4th N. Y. Cavalry*

Colonel Cesnola is a Sardinian of noble family, and was educated in the best military schools of Europe, having been placed in that at Paris when only nine years of age. His father was at that time Secretary of War under the Sardinian government. The son came to this country just before the breaking out of the rebellion, and hostilities quickly elicited his enthusiastic interest in the cause of the Union. Having had experience in the Crimean war, as a member of the staff of the Sardinian General-in-chief, he was well qualified for the duties of the field. In September, 1862, he took command of the 4th N.Y. Cavalry, whose superior discipline and many brave achievements have gained for it an enviable fame. At the battle of Aldie, June, 1863, he was commended for his gallant conduct by General Kilpatrick, early in the action, but afterwards, while far in the advance, he was surrounded by superior numbers, and taken prisoner. He spent ten months in Libby prison. After his exchange he returned to his regiment, and led the brigade to which it belonged in many severe engagements previous to its mustering out, in September last(. . .) Soon after entering Libby, the rebel officer in charge, offered Colonel Cesnola, with some other *foreigners,* better quarters than their fellow officers had, which proposal was indignantly rejected. "We are U. S. officers," they said.

I entered the service of the United States in October, 1861, and was captured in Virginia the 17th of June, 1863, at the cavalry engagement of Aldie.[1] I was marched, mostly on foot, more than one hundred miles to Staunton, and thence by railroad conveyed to the rebel capital and confined in the Libby prison. I arrived in Richmond the 25th of June, at about four o'clock in the afternoon, and remained immured in that tobacco factory until the 24th of March, 1864, when I was specially exchanged for Colonel Brown of the 59th Georgia, regiment.

Searching for valuables

At my arrival in Libby I was called into the office of the commanding officer of that military prison, Captain (now Major) Thos. P. Turner, and by him, my name, rank, regiment, etc., was registered in his book; the walls of Turner's office were covered with captured U. S. colors, regimental battle flags, and cavalry guidons. From that office I was ordered into a spacious dark hall, in a corner of which, a rebel sergeant searched me through from head to foot, in the roughest manner possible. He took away from me every little trinket I had, my penknife, eyeglasses, meerschaum-pipe, matches, and a bunch of small keys; and was angry because he could not find any greenbacks on my person. He ordered me to take off my boots for inspection; I answered him that I always had a servant to perform that service for me. He insisted, but I refused until he took them off himself, and searched them very minutely. He asked me what I had done with my money, and if I had any watch. I told him that a chivalric Southron had stolen my watch and money during the march from Middleburg to Staunton. He began to abuse me, using very profane language and denying my veracity. I told him that perhaps the gentleman intended only to borrow those articles from me. Captain Fisher, a signal officer of the Army of the Potomac, was punished and kept walking for several hours with the sentinel at the prison's door simply for not giving up immediately his India rubber coat, which he justly claimed as his own private property. I entered therefore the gates of a Confederate prison stripped of everything except my spurs, which being screwed into the boots could not be removed. I remained in this deplorable condition, without a book to read, or a sheet of paper to write, for over five months, nursing my grief during the whole day, using my boots for a pillow during the night, and sleeping on the bare and often damp plank floor, with neither blanket nor overcoat, nor any other covering. Dogs had certainly better sleeping accommodations in their kennels than I had there. In the same wretched condition, however, were many other officers. We were compelled for several months to wash and scrub the floor, the kitchen, the tables and the sinks ourselves, and I cannot recollect but with feelings of admiration the serenity of countenance with which I saw our present Adjutant General of the State, Brigadier General W. Irvine (at that time Lieutenant Colonel of the 10th New York Cavalry), in shirt sleeves, scrubbing the floor when it was his turn to do so. I must confess such service was revolting to me, and I always found some good-hearted fellow prisoner who, for sake of exercise, would perform it in my stead. It may have been a mere chance, but it was precisely when the officers were performing such menial services that the Southern ladies would come to have a peep at the Yankees, who certainly were not looking at that moment to their best advantage. I had but one single shirt during four months, and when I washed it, I looked more like a Roman Gladiator of olden times than a Colonel in the United States service.

Rations

From June up to September, we had for ration the half of an ordinary sized loaf of wheat bread, tolerably good, though often sour. It is very true that the beans were of the poorest kind, in each of which there was the nest of an insect; and the small ration of meat tough, and not of the best quality; but hunger had no law, and I would swallow my ration, bad as it was, longing afterwards for that of my neighbor also. In the rooms where we were, no chairs could be seen, nor benches; in fact, nothing but the bare walls and the bare floor, with the exception of some boards roughly joined together in form of tables, at which one-tenth only of the prisoners could eat at a time. After September, our ration was considerably reduced in quality and quantity, and we received half a loaf of negro made corn bread, so hard that it was called by our officers *iron clad*, *solid shot*, *railroad iron*, etc., and some few ounces of meat, four or five times per month.

Inspector of prisons

Richard Turner (no relation of Major Turner), a Marylander by birth, and a porter (I am told) by occupation, at the outbreaking of this war at the Eutaw House in the City of Baltimore, is the inspector of the Libby and of other military prisons in Richmond. So much has been said of the ferocity of this man by the press and by the testimony of other officers, that I have nothing to add. I wish I could lighten the heavy burden of misdeeds with which his name goes to posterity. As to myself, personally, he has never done any harm, but rather tried to do good.

He used to come into our rooms at different hours during the day, and if he could catch any officer sitting or lying on his blankets he would confiscate them for the use of his own horses. I was present one day when he caught Captain King, of the 12th Pennsylvania cavalry, spitting on the floor (he simply missed a box which was used as a spittoon), and he brought him down into a dungeon and kept him there for forty-eight hours, on bread and water.

Sanitary Commission

Early in October intelligence was received at the Libby that the United States Sanitary Commission and our government had sent us a large quantity of boxes, containing blankets and other articles of clothing, etc. I made at once an application to get two blankets for my personal use. It was not, however, until the beginning of the next month that I succeeded in getting them, one to sleep on, and the other to cover me with. These blankets were issued to me by my friend and fellow prisoner, Brigadier General Neal Dow, who had been appointed by the rebel Colonel Ould, commissioner of exchange of prisoners of war, as commissary of distribution.

Commissary of distribution

The 10th of November, 1863, late in the afternoon, I was called downstairs in Major Turner's office, and informed by him that I was selected to supersede General Neal Dow as commissary of distribution, whose appointment was obnoxious to General J. H. Winder, Military Governor of Richmond. I was informed that the selection was made on account of my being the next senior officer to the General. He further intimated that I would not be allowed to hold conversation with our men on Belle Isle, nor carry any verbal or written communication from the officers to the men, or vice versa, without previously submitting such communication to the rebel officer in command of the island, and of other personal restrictions. After having promised to comply with such orders, I was allowed to select amongst the field officers, two assistants, subject to the approval of General Winder. I selected Lieutenant Colonel Boyd, and my friend, Lieutenant Colonel Von Schrader, Inspector General of the 14th Army corps; both of whom were approved. The next morning Richard Turner, under whose control were all boxes sent from the North, informed me that he would not send the boxes of clothing down to Belle Isle if I did not pay the transportation for them. I had not one cent of my own, but Colonel Boyd had some funds in the rebel hands and offered to pay with that money the transportation; and after a day's delay it was accepted. We were allowed to go to Belle Isle at 10 A.M. every morning, and remain there until 4 o'clock P.M. Two policemen would accompany, or rather escort us from the Libby to Belle Isle, and from thence back to the prison, every day.

Belle Isle

On the 13th of November there were at Belle Isle six thousand four hundred and thirty-four Union soldiers as prisoners of war. I do not describe here the place, as I see it is pretty correctly done by Colonel Farnsworth, of the 1st Connecticut cavalry, in his testimony.

Lieutenant Bossieux, the officer in charge of that prison camp, was well spoken of universally, and I must confess that I found him gentlemanly, humane and generous-hearted. His name, however, shows his foreign origin, though he may have been born in Richmond. Every facility in his power was cheerfully afforded me for the distribution of the United States Sanitary Commission's goods, as well as for those sent by our government. Our prisoners there, were divided into squads of one hundred men, each under the command of a sergeant, (fellow-prisoner) who was responsible to the rebel commander for the behavior of his men. This camp was therefore divided into sixty-four squads, augmenting the number of the squads in proportion to the arrival of prisoners there.

Distribution of blankets, clothing, etc.

We were permitted by Major Turner to see and count the number of boxes piled up in a warehouse near the Libby, and make a rough calculation of the quantity of each article of clothing contained in those boxes. The most necessary thing for those poor men were blankets; so we decided to distribute them without delay, but the number was too small to provide every man with one, so we gave a blanket to every two men. In the progress of distribution, the arrival of many more boxes from Fortress Monroe, enabled us to issue one to each man. The modus operandi was the following: Colonel Von Schrader, with a Union soldier as a clerk, would take one squad outside of the enclosure on what was, by the rebels, called "the parade ground," and put down the name of each man and all the articles of clothing he needed into blank rolls sent us by the U. S. government for that purpose; Colonel Boyd and myself would likewise have each one a squad and a prisoner as clerk, to write down names and articles needed, in the same manner.

This method was only continued for the first two days, while we were awaiting the arrival of the boxes from Richmond. But as soon as we received a sufficient number of them, Colonel Boyd being a quartermaster, consented to distribute the articles, while Colonel Von Schrader and myself continued taking down the names and articles wanted by the men. We used to inspect about eight squads a day; the distributing officer, however, could not proceed so fast, as he had to open the boxes, etc; the average of squads furnished per day was three, that is three hundred men. The greatest part of the day was lost in going from Richmond to Belle Isle, and returning. Sometimes the boatman was not there to convey us to the other side of the James river, and much precious time was thus lost. I endeavored to obtain permission to sleep at Belle

Isle, in order to be at work early in the morning in distributing, as the cold weather was terribly felt by our poor men. But Major Turner had no power to grant this, and having asked General Winder if an application to him in writing, signed by the Committee of Distribution, would be taken into consideration, his brutish answer was, "*No, certainly not.*"

Besides the time lost in going and coming back and waiting for the boat, we lost much time there also, as the squads, when called out by us, were sometimes receiving their rations; at another they were at roll-call, etc. So we could not transact business really more than three hours every day, which retarded the distribution considerably, while we would have very willingly distributed day and night in order to shelter with good warm clothes the thousands of half naked bodies, shivering from head to foot from cold and hunger. I am a soldier by profession since my boyhood; I have been in several wars in Europe; I am familiar with death, and have seen it in all its different aspects, but my heart has never been moved as it was by the condition of those men at Belle Isle. Their frozen feet wrapped in a piece of blanket or an old flannel shirt, in place of the boots which were taken away from them by their captors, those long, pale, hungry faces, with hair and beard uncut for months; a kind of perpetual motion given to their bodies by the millions of vermin that devoured their very flesh; their emaciated forms, telling at first sight how many long and weary, weary months they had been there fighting against death in the form of scurvy, low fevers, diarrhea, congestion of the lungs, etc.; their feeble voices saying, "Oh! Colonel, do give us something to eat, for God's sake," etc. These scenes, I confess, were to me heartrending in the extreme. These men received at meal time, one bucket of broken pieces of corn bread, and one bucket of over-boiled sweet potatoes for every one hundred men! I saw it myself many times! Indeed, it was so revolting that I think even pigs would have sickened at it. How the chiefs of squads could divide so small a quantity of food in one hundred parts has always been for me a problem, which I am still unable to solve; though often, while distributing the clothing, some men would come to me and complain that for whole days they could not get anything to eat, because before their turn came the bucket was empty!

It was no wonder if these poor, starved human beings would eat rats and dogs. I recollect the fact of a rebel officer having gone inside the inclosure to visit the prisoners, accompanied by a dog. He did not miss it until he was coming out; but, alas! it was too late, and by that time he could only see one man gnawing with voracity his dog's last bone! The next day the *Richmond Enquirer*, edited by that Irish patriot, John Mitchell, had a leading article entitled, "Dogs eat Dogs," and gave the particulars of the affair, summing up by saying that the Yankee prisoners at Belle Isle, though furnished with plenty of wholesome food, preferred to eat dogs.

Of these six thousand four hundred and thirty-four prisoners, over seven hundred were at the time I first visited Belle Isle, without tents or any shelter whatever at night, lying in ditches, or digging holes in the sandy ground in which they slept in a bundle, one over the other, and I heard that often in the morning those who were on the top were found frozen to death, and I actually saw men wrapped up in blankets brought out of the enclosure who were found dead and frozen in ditches outside of the tents!

Upon this subject I had frequent conversations with Lieutenant Bossieux, who told me himself he had several times made proper requisitions for the necessary tents; that he went to see the quartermaster of the prison himself (an Ohio renegade, was a greater scoundrel than any of the Southern race); that they were promised but never delivered. He also told me he had made a plan for barracks which would have cost very little and would have accommodated our men all comfortably, but that he never heard anything more about it, nor of boards given for that or any other purpose. After having distributed the contents of several boxes, I perceived that the empty boxes were, by order of Lieutenant Bossieux piled up as if to be used for some purpose. I went to see him, and told him I intended to give to the men those empty boxes, so that they could floor their tents with them. He said he had instructions from the quartermaster to save all those boxes, that he wanted them to pack army clothing in, but he would give me in return the boards necessary to floor all the tents. I said nothing further for three or four days, but seeing that the boards were coming only in the same manner as the tents so many times asked, I took upon myself, at the cost of being superseded for it, not to wait any longer, and I distributed them to the men, gladdening many hearts. A portion of these boxes were used to make coffins for those who had ceased to suffer in this wicked place.

Plundering

There has been so much said about the rebel government stealing half the boxes sent to us by the government, and the United States Sanitary Commission, that I have recalled to my memory all the minutest particulars which have reference to them, and I have come to the conclusion that the largest number of the boxes of clothing were turned over to us for distribution, and that they had no official connection with the heavy robberies which we have unfortunately sustained, and were unable to prevent.

Richmond City battalions

It is true that the Richmond City battalions, who guarded the federal prisoners, had a large number of their men clothed in U.S. uniforms, but my opinions (I may be wrong) is, that the warehouse adjacent to the Libby, in which all our boxes were stored and guarded by them, was visited at night by these undisciplined and unprincipled soldiery, who would appropriate to themselves and sell to others, all the clothing they wanted. I came to this conclusion, after I had visited that warehouse several times, as I found ragged rebel uniforms left here and there in the corners of the warehouse; showing plainly that some of the rebels had made their hasty toilet there. When one hundred and nine Union officers escaped from the Libby, through the tunnel, I had the scurvy and could not join the party. The next morning I conversed with some of the sentinels, and laughed at their great vigilance during the previous night. They said that they had seen men coming out from the yard of the warehouse, and running as fast as they could, but they supposed *it was some of their own guard making a raid on our boxes*. Several times in the stillness of the night, I heard plainly in the warehouse the hammering and breaking of boxes, but this was the robbers' midnight work, and scarcely chargeable to the rebel authorities. The rebel government was, however, guilty of the grossest indifference as to the safe keeping of our boxes; of that there is no doubt, but I cannot bring myself to believe that their authorities were officially connected with it.

The boxes sent from Richmond to Belle Isle for immediate distribution, were also plundered during the night, even after I obtained permission to put some of our own men to guard them. Our hungry men, tempted by the sentinels with bread and pies, would give a portion of the clothing issued to them, for both or either of them; and, as in all large communities, there were amongst our prisoners some rascals who would steal the clothing of their sleeping comrades and sell them likewise to the guard. Colonel Von Schrader and myself remonstrated several times to Lieutenant Bossieux, and he put several of his men in irons for having bought clothing from our prisoners, but the evil could not be stopped by us.

I have often been present at guard mounting in Belle Isle, and remarked the relieved party (sometimes half of them) would have either U. S. blankets, overcoats or pantaloons, and the relieving party of that day would come off duty the next morning similarly supplied with new U. S. clothes. These facts, of course, not being generally known to our fellow prisoners, and from the barred windows of the Libby seeing a very large number of the guard dressed in U. S. uniforms, they came to the very natural conclusion that the rebel government was robbing us to clothe their own men.

The rebel authorities have never given to Colonel Boyd or Colonel Von Schrader or myself (that I am aware of,) the invoices which, I suppose both the government and the U. S. Sanitary Commission must have sent with the goods. I asked Major Turner if he had those invoices; he replied he had not seen them. I inquired also of Richard Turner in regard to them, but he rudely told me that it was not my business. From this reason I was unable to find out how many boxes were sent to us.

Making shoes

My narrative now soon comes to a close. Towards the latter part of November I was superseded as Commissary of Distribution by order of General J. H. Winder. Two causes originated it. The first was this: the rebels came one day to Belle Isle, and paroled four hundred men to make shoes for their army, and intimated that they would come again in a few days to parole several hundred more for the same object. I decided at once to do what I considered the duty of a U. S. officer, and interfere in this matter. I sent for several of the chiefs of squads, and told them to inform the men that by going to work for the rebels they were breaking their oath towards the U. S. government, and were helping instead of fighting the enemy of their country; that they would be all liable to be court-martialed for it as soon as they reached our lines, and that I considered it my duty to inform them of it. These sergeants went at once to see their men, and the result was that when the rebels came the second time, they could not get a single one, and soon they discovered the reason for it.

The second cause for which I was superseded is the following. One morning, rather earlier than usual, we were ordered out of our room for the purpose of having it scrubbed by the negroes. The overseer who had charge of the negroes (always with a stick in his hands), came to the corner where I had my quarters, and two buckets of water were thrown on the floor by his negroes before I was aware of their presence. In the haste of leaving the room my friend and messmate, Lieutenant Morley, of the 12th Pennsylvania cavalry, had left a piece of ham on the shelf, within reach of any unscrupulous hand which chose to take it. I called him back and told him to put it out of reach, as I was as much afraid of negro thieves as of white ones. The overseer, whom I had not perceived was behind me, heard the remark and applied the meaning to himself. To my surprise he put one hand on my shoulder and made use of the following language: "God d–m you, do you mean that I am a thief?" If a hot iron had touched my skin it would not have maddened me more than his insolent touch did. I turned myself towards me, and in a second I had him by the throat with both my hands, down he went on the floor, and I struck him many times as hard as I could on his face, until my rage was satisfied. The negroes were jubilant, and of course nobody interfered to help the overseer. I was called downstairs in Major Turner's office, where I explained the whole affair, and though I was not punished bodily, my supersedure took place on that very morning.

From November to March, 1864, I was not allowed to leave for a single moment the Libby prison, and when they began to parole and send North some officers, all the other colonels but two were sent North before me; though I had been a prisoner longer than any of them. Colonel Robert Ould, the rebel Commissioner, to whom I was obnoxious, said that he did not want to send me North at all, but he would keep me in prison as long as he liked; but he was nevertheless soon afterwards compelled to send me, as Colonel Jack Brown, of the 59th Georgia regiment was sent South conditionally, that if he could not get me exchanged for him, he was to return North and be kept as long as I was held by the rebel authorities.

MONACA O STREGA?

The Catholic Missionary as Outsider in Sister Blandina Segale's
At the End of the Santa Fe Trail

Reading Sister Blandina Segale's journal *At the End of the Santa Fe Trail* (written between 1872 and 1893, published as a book in 1932), one is more likely to be struck by the extraordinary, larger-than-life character of some of the experiences narrated by the author, than by the book's significance as an early example of Italian American autobiography. Almost inevitably, the reader's attention focuses on what this nun (she was a "Sister of Charity") saw and went through during her twenty years of missionary work on the frontier of Colorado and New Mexico, rather than on her origins. Nonetheless, the opening of *At the End*, where we get a glimpse of the young Blandina (born Rosa Maria) interacting with her parents and some of their close friends, is quite important for our understanding of her personality.

In the first pages of the book one has a distinct sensation of the thrill Segale experiences at the news that she is to resign her teaching duties at Steubenville, Ohio, and leave alone for a mission in the mining town of Trinidad, Colorado. One also notices, by contrast, her trepidation at the prospect of spending a day with her family in Cincinnati prior to her departure. She confides to her journal that she anticipates "a scene" (7), and her tone has a surprisingly apprehensive quality (something one rarely detects in the rest of the book).[1]

Segale's recreation of her last day at home is effective. Her narration enables us to visualize the comings and goings of family friends, to listen to their overlapping voices, and to sense the pressure that this close-knit community exercises upon those who want to affirm their independence. From the point of view of her father and, in general, of the small Italian colony of Cincinnati, Segale's behavior represents an anomaly, a departure from established customs. They react with a mixture of incredulity and resentment to her firm resolve to comply with her superiors' orders. Her mother, on the contrary, shows great respect for her convictions and does not try to deter her from her purpose.

The fact that, as a religious person, she has already renounced her family, does not appear to be considered by those who argue against her choice. To them she remains simply a young woman, a daughter who has inexplicably decided to violate the unity of the family. In the eyes of her father, her unwavering commitment to the Church assumes the painful significance of an extreme form of commitment to the self, a willful act of disobedience.

> After mother had a short interview with me, father managed to see me alone. He took hold of me and asked, "Have I ever denied you anything?"
> I signified no.
> "You have never disobeyed me in your life?"
> I assented.
> "Now I command you – you must not go on this far away mission! Are you going?"
> "Yes, father." He let go the hold on my arm and walked toward the door. Not without my seeing his tears falling fast. He did not realize his hold on my arm gave me pain – not to speak of the heart-pain for him. (8)

To some of the people she meets while traveling through the West, the narrator of *At the End* is an enigma. They respond with perplexity, and even distrust, to her unusual appearance (her black garb), her behavior, or both. They grasp that she is not an "ordinary woman," but cannot quite define or "classify" her. She does not fit the conventional categories of femininity:

> In the railway station at St. Louis between train time, I got off to purchase a pair of arctics. I saw several Italian women selling fruit. One of them had a daughter standing near. I asked the mother if she would permit her daughter to accompany me to the shoe store, which was in sight. The mother looked at me earnestly than said to her neighbor peddler, "How do I know who she is, she looks like a *monaca* (sister) but she might be a *strega* (witch)." (9)

Later in the narrative it is Segale herself who, having displayed uncommon courage and fearlessness in a situation of danger, muses that the men around her must "think I'm either a saint or a witch" (179). And the choice of such alternative identities should not surprise us. As Marcello Craveri has suggested, saints and witches are by no means totally different types of women (7-62). Traditionally, they both stand for "extreme" forms of behavior; they are transgressors of the limits society has imposed upon women. On another occasion, it is a good-natured cowboy who, having met Segale on a train bound for Colorado, expresses his uncertainty about her identity by asking "what kind of a lady" (25) she is. One suspects that her self-assurance and resourcefulness strike him as incongruous with her gender. And indeed, according to the standards of her society and time, Segale's willingness to travel alone in the West is a most "unwomanly" display of imprudence. Not less significant is an episode in which the nuns of a Kansas City convent, after learning that Segale is traveling unaccompanied, suspect her of being an impostor (13-15).

In the times and places described in *At the End*, a nun's habit could appear curious or even sinister to those who were not acquainted with its religious meaning. To be sure, Segale was well aware of the theatrical quality of her dress and often describes the impression it made on those who met her, were they Native Americans, settlers, or outlaws. Its significance for her, however, went well beyond its simple appearance. One has almost the impression, at times, that Segale conceived of her black dress and her very identity as a single thing. It is not accidental, I think, that *At the End* opens and closes with episodes in which someone attempts to divest Segale – both literally and symbolically – of her religious garb.

During Segale's last visit to her household, to which we referred earlier, a friend threatens to remove her habit, thereby forcing her to remain at home. It is an attempt to remind her that she is a daughter before she is a nun. In the last pages of the journal we read of how the public school authorities of Colorado inform Segale that she could continue to teach only if she consented to discard her habit. In both instances it is as if the black dress were seen as the source of her strength and independence, as a sort of magic object without which Segale would turn into an "ordinary" woman, an obedient daughter, a docile employee. But Segale clung to her "uniform," even at the cost of inflicting pain on those she loved, or of resigning from a school she had helped to establish.

Segale's emphasis on the importance and symbolic value of her habit, signals that she identified more deeply with her worship than with her background and origins, or with the country where she lived. Being Catholic came before being a native Italian (she was born in Cicagna, in the region of Liguria) or a U. S. citizen. This is not to suggest, of course, that one may ignore the fragments of *italianità* scattered throughout the text. Segale's references to such authors as Dante, Tasso, and Manzoni, or her preference for the adjective "Italian" over regional qualifiers (the latter being so common in later Italian American memoirs)[2] bespeaks a surprising sense of national culture (especially if we consider that the journal was begun only two years after Italy's unification). Yet it is also true that the world of her parents and the memories of her birthplace do not seem to play as great a role in her everyday experience as her loyalty to the Catholic Church and her dedication to her work. She tells us, for example, that her mother's native dialect strikes her as something which, though familiar, is removed in time and place ("it was like hearing sketches of a favorite opera" [8]). It is evoked as a sound, as a form of music, rather than as a form of communication.

Presenting *At the End*, Helen Barolini has pointed out that in Segale's time "Italians [in the U. S.] were so few and far between that there was no developed prejudice against them" (*Dream* 5). Being Italian, or of Italian descent, did not necessarily mean (as it would in later years) being part of a minority whose image had to be defended against the distortions and stereotypes circulated by the dominant culture. Being Catholic, on the other hand, certainly meant belonging to a community traditionally regarded with suspicion and hostility by the Protestant majority. It was about her Catholicity, not about her "Italianness," that Segale had to be defensive.

Despite the private character of *At the End* (it was originally meant to have only one reader, the author's sister Justina), Segale comes across as a determined and, at times, even pugnacious champion of Catholicism and its role and presence in the West. Her words often convey the impression that she is moving in enemy territory and that the value of her efforts (and those of the other Catholic missionaries) has to be constantly upheld and vindicated. What makes the West "enemy territory" is not, as it might be supposed, its "wildness" or lawlessness, nor the "danger" supposedly posed by some Native American tribes, but rather the attitude of the dominant culture, the culture of white, Anglo-Saxon, and – most importantly – Protestant America. It is an oppressive and destructive attitude which, as Segale realizes early on, finds expression in the attempt to marginalize and silence all that is other. And it is as a Catholic that she identifies with the plight of minorities. As a Catholic, she writes in the name of marginality. And when one recognizes in her writing that "necessity" to explain oneself to others that is an almost inescapable part of the Italian American – or Mexican American, Asian American – experience (Tamburri et al., *Margin* 5), what is explained is invariably her faith rather than her ethnicity.

Exemplary, in this sense, is a conversation Segale holds with a young Protestant missionary on a train, at the outset of her journey to Trinidad, Colorado. Asked about her salary and her motivations, Segale replies as follows:

> "It is very simple to any Catholic. He or she makes application for admittance into a religious community and offers himself or herself to give service to God. The service rendered is according to the rules and constitutions of the Order for which he or she feels called. After we have tested ourselves and superiors have tested us, we, of our own will, bind ourselves by sacred promises – one of which, in our community, is not to use money for personal use – only for the good of others. Do you not think that a sure investment?"
>
> "Do you mean you work all your life and give the money to others?"
>
> "You are clothing my meaning with new words, but it amounts to the same." (12)

By explaining her worship and what her vocation implies, Segale explains and defines herself as well. The distinctive didactic quality that characterizes her tone here as in other passages is a direct response to anti-Catholic prejudice. *At the End* is, among other things, an attempt to counteract the dominant culture's discrimination against and misrepresentation of Catholicism.

Segale frequently insists, in the narrative, that Catholics in the West tell their own story. As she explains with lucidity, they cannot possibly count on the establishment for a complete and truthful account of their work and accomplishments. With her journal (which she did, eventually, agree to publish), Segale sets a powerful example of how to find one's voice, of how to break the silence. What is more, her voice is a voice for all the weak, all the oppressed. It is a voice that unhesitatingly denounces Anglo-Saxon racism toward the Spanish-speaking inhabitants of Colorado and New Mexico, and the "extermination" (263) of the "rightful possessors of the [American] soil" (52), the Indians.

The strategy of Segale's passionate defense of the Hispanics consists in subverting the "us vs. them" discourse generated by the dominant culture. In the pages of her journal it is the settlers and their government that become "other." Presented from the point of view of the Hispanics, the "men from the States" (235) are thus labeled as "strangers," "invading fortune hunters," "land-sharpers," "land-grabbers," "sharks," "despoilers," "violators of 'Thou shalt not steal,'" and "corrupters of the Spanish language" (45-46). Of all these terms, "land-grabbers" is the one that appears most frequently in the text. And although Segale explains at some point that those she designates by that word are not "representative Americans" (161), the impact of its continuous repetition is overwhelming: it places the Hispanics in the role of victims and North Americans in that of perpetrators.

In Segale's representation, the culture of the Spanish-speaking population of the West is a rich and sophisticated one, whose value the settlers fail – or choose not – to recognize and respect. They show no appreciation for the Hispanics' "innate refinement" (38, 229), elegant manners, and "natural culture" (229), displaying only aggressiveness and contempt in their attitude toward them (an attitude exemplified by the racial slurs Segale mentions in the text: "greasers," "coyotes," or "kangaroos").

But even more destructive, as we are often reminded, is the settlers' behavior toward the original inhabitants of the continent. Dealing with them on the basis of a sort of brutal Darwinism ("that English phrase, 'The survival of the fittest,' is being applied to the rightful owners of this country." [262]), they have activated an irreversible process that, in Segale's view, can only lead to the annihilation of all Native Americans: "Poor, poor Indians! they are doomed to lose. Then will come strict adherence to reservation rules – then diminution of numbers, and then extinction" (302).

The narrator's treatment of the "Indian question" in *At the End* may be described as part of that philanthropic and humanitarian tradition of the second half of the nineteenth century which Roy Harvey Pearce has discussed in *Savagism and Civilization*. Like the authors Pearce refers to (Henry Schoolcraft and Helen Hunt Jackson, 241), Segale insistently and fervently promotes the idea that Native Americans need to be safeguarded ("contacts made by me with any Indian tribe were, and are, of a protective type" [331]). As portrayed in *At the End*, Native Americans lack not only the strength but also – and crucially – a real awareness of their enemies' determination and ruthlessness. They are astonished and outraged at the duplicity of the government agents who use every possible means to deprive them of their territories. They fail to realize that what is happening is simply that, as Segale puts it, "the conquerors claim the land" (41). What, in my view, partially redeems Segale's paternalism, is the utter conviction with which she denounces the terrible consequences of white expansionism. If, on the one hand, she presents Native Americans as helpless victims, "unevolved minds" (52) that need to be educated and civilized, on the other we are also told that:

> Generations to come will blush for the deeds of this, toward the rightful possessors of the soil. Our government, which opposes with upraised finger of scorn any act which savors of tyranny, lowers that finger to crush out of existence a race whose right to the land we call America is unquestioned. (52)

To be sure, Segale's view that Native Americans can "advance" as human beings with the aid of education and religion is far from revolutionary. Rather surprising, instead, is what she envisages as the result of such progress. For what her "educated and civilized" Native American can aspire to become is not, as one might expect, a "model citizen," someone who may be painlessly assimilated into white culture, but rather nothing less than "the ideal man" (236). He or she may reach, in other words, a state of excellence Segale imagines as far superior to that of Anglo-American society. While Segale unhesitatingly maintains that Native Americans have "the vices of barbarism" (236), she at the same time gives us a portrayal of their enemies which is hardly a tribute to white civilization. She shows us repeatedly how violence can be found on both sides, so that, in a sense, the very separation between the traditional categories of "barbarism" and "civilization" becomes blurred.

Segale is also able, occasionally, to abandon her generalizations about "the Indian" in favor of precise observations on specific tribes – such as the Utes, the Apaches, the Comanches, and the Kiowas – and their various cultures. The philanthropist gives way to the keen observer and annotator of foreign customs and the "rightful possessors of the soil" cease, however temporarily, to be simply an abstract image.

This is particularly true of the story of the Ute chief Rafael, possibly the journal's most eloquent entry on the relationship between different cultures and worldviews:

> Rafael continued: "*Nana, tu hijo esta muerto*" (Mother, your son is dead), Rafael made the motion of pouring water on the head, wanting me to understand that his son had been baptized. He continued: "When one of us dies, we move camp. Will you bury him?" The missionaries called the members of a tribe "children," hence, Rafael said: "*Tu hijo*" (your son) is dead . . .
>
> Ahead of this funeral cortege came William Anderson, one of the three who went for the dead Indian. He left the procession and hastily came into the temporary mortuary chapel and said: "Sister, you have been imposed upon. The young Eagle lives."
>
> I responded: "Surely, William, there is a misinterpretation of words somewhere."
>
> He continued: "No, Sister, he is sick, but not dead . . .
>
> I questioned Chief Rafael.
>
> "Did you not say to me, '*Tu hijo esta muerto*'?" (Your son is dead).
>
> "*Si, Nana.*" (Yes, mother).
>
> "But this gentleman says he is ill, not dead."
>
> "Oh, Nana, he is dead. I tell you he is dead. I will carry him in to let you see he is dead."
>
> Rafael carried the young man into the room and stood him before me. The agonizing patient could not stand, and the father caught him before he fell . . . The young man died in the afternoon and was buried as became one who had been regenerated by the waters of holy baptism.
>
> Still, I was anxious to know why Rafael called his son's condition death, so I asked him, "When do you say an Indian is dead?" "When he has no heart. You saw, Nana, he had no heart when I carried him to let you see him." Meaning, his son had given up hopes of living and had no pulse, which he called heart. He knew no other way of expressing his meaning, "no heart," means death. (52-55)

Segale's sympathetic portrayal of Billy the Kid, whom she claimed to have met on three different occasions,[3] is further evidence of her tendency to identify with the outsider's perspective. As presented in *At the End*, he is more a victim than a villain, being but the natural offspring of a land where the notion of legality is largely unknown. While not downplaying in the least his reputation as "the greatest murderer of the Southwest" (209), Segale at the same time distances herself from his antagonists, namely the representatives of "law and order." In the America she describes the authorities not only tolerate, but contribute to, the general predominance of brutality and violence. Inevitably then, they lack the moral stature to be creditable guarantors of justice and truth.

As narrated by Segale, the story of Billy and his gang becomes a story of wasted lives, of a tragic loss of youth, intelligence, and ardor ("Think, dear Sister Justina, how many crimes might have been prevented, had someone had influence over 'Billy' after his first murder" [208]). It is the indictment of a culture that places little value upon human life, a culture the narrator of *At the End* plainly does not feel to be her own.

> Poor, poor "Billy the Kid," was shot by Sheriff Patrick F. Garrett of Lincoln County. That ends the career of one who began his downward course at the age of twelve years by taking revenge for the insult that had been offered to his mother... Only now have I learned his proper name – William H. Bonney. (224-225)

Whether dealing with minorities or, as in this case, with its dissident sons, the establishment seems only able to express itself through the language of might and violence. To this Segale opposes her firm commitment to dialogue as a means of bridging the distance between different cultures, mentalities and ethics. The numerous conversations "recreated" in the journal give ample proof of her ability to tailor her discourse to the character and social level of her interlocutors. At the same time, through the example of her activities in

Colorado and New Mexico, she suggests a possible role for Catholic missionaries in the West as cultural mediators and defenders of the subaltern. Written by a nun, by a woman with a foreign-sounding name, *At the End of the Santa Fe Trail* may be described, then, as a call for solidarity and resistance. Rather than the journal of an American Catholic, it should be called the journal of a Catholic in America.

A "LOST SOUL" IN AMERICA

Emanuel Carnevali's Autobiography

A "lost soul" is the expression William Carlos Williams used in his autobiography (266) to describe Emanuel Carnevali (1897-1942), the expatriate poet and prose writer who, from the late 1910s to the early 1920s, flashed like a meteor across the scene of modern American literature. Born in Florence, he left his native Italy for the United States at the age of sixteen (in 1914). Stranded in New York with no money, he had survived doing odd jobs (mostly in cheap restaurants and bars), had rapidly learned English, and had found his vocation in writing. In the relatively short time he spent in the States – eight years in all – his literary activity brought him in contact with some of the country's most interesting and influential writers and editors. In addition to Williams, he was associated at one time or another with the likes of Carl Sandburg, Sherwood Anderson, Harriet Monroe, Waldo Frank, and Robert McAlmon, whose Paris press, Contact Editions, issued his collection of tales, poems, and essays *A Hurried Man* in 1925 (the only book Carnevali published during his lifetime).

Carnevali's writings appeared in such magazines as *Others*, *The Little Review*, and *Poetry*. Of this last publication he became Associate Editor in 1919, when he transferred from New York to Chicago. It was there that he experienced the first symptoms of the terrible disease – encephalitis lethargica (a devastating form of sleeping sickness) – that brought his

American experience to an end. Sent back to Italy for treatment in 1922, he spent his final years almost constantly in bed, in hospitals, sanatoriums, or in miserable rooms, where he continued to write in spite of the terrible shaking fits that seized him when he was conscious. Even though the "American" part of his life was over, he continued to write in English. The language that had once given expression to a young expatriate's experiences, hopes, and rage, thus became the language of his nightmares and visions, and, most importantly, of memory.

To reconsider Carnevali's writings is to discover that, notwithstanding its tragic, untimely conclusion, his life story was one of heroic affirmation. I see his autobiography as a powerful testimony of a victory over silence and oblivion, of the triumphant appropriation of the language of 20th-century America by a foreign-born artist. It is a text that reconstructs a unique experience and provides at the same time a compressed but poignant rendering of the immigrant story.

In a letter of 1919 to Italian author Giovanni Papini – whose life and works were a major source of inspiration for him – Carnevali mentions that he began to write in English when he was nineteen and adds: "I will remain in America to write. This is my country"[1] (*America* 91). In a way, I think, these words hold true, even though we know that, physically, he was forced to go back to Italy. By choosing to tell his story in English, Carnevali never really left America, as an author – he never really ceased to be an American writer. At times he may have felt he did not quite belong there (in another letter to Papini he writes: "they like me and admire me here, but I am the foreigner" [*America* 99]), but I believe this did not interfere with his view of himself as a writer of that country. Indeed, that conviction perfectly accorded with the feeling of being an outsider, of living on the margins of American society.

Back in Italy, Carnevali intended to write his autobiography, or an autobiographical novel, and wanted to call it *The First God* or *Religious Stammering* or *The White Man*. The first six chapters of what was still a work in progress appeared in the 1932 anthology *Americans Abroad*, edited by Peter Neagoe (73-82). Carnevali died in 1942 without completing his work, but his papers were collected, compiled and edited by Kay Boyle, with whom he had corresponded during his final years. The book came out only in 1967 with the title *The Autobiography of Emanuel Carnevali*. It includes not only the unfinished narrative of Carnevali's life, but also some of his stories, essays, and poems, and might be appropriately called the "portable Carnevali."[2] An Italian-language version, entitled *Il Primo Dio* ("The First God"), was published in 1978. Edited by Emanuel's half-sister Maria Pia Carnevali, with the help of a Carnevali devotee and scholar, David Stivender, this version presents a different arrangement of some of the early chapters, it leaves out the additional material inserted by Kay Boyle in her edition, and claims to adhere more strictly to the author's original plan.[3] Although the English-language version calls itself an autobiography, whereas the Italian translation is presented as a work of fiction, both works are better described as partaking of the two genres. The phrase Paul John Eakin has used to define William Maxwell's *So Long, See You Tomorrow* (1980), perfectly fits both *The Autobiography of Emanuel Carnevali* and *Il Primo Dio*: "a narrative with equal claims to being a memoir and a novel (it is both)" (6).

All major studies on Carnevali contain some sort of notice explaining that both printed versions of his unfinished narrative are reconstructions, and that the same could be said of *A Hurried Man*, which Robert McAlmon assembled and edited while Carnevali was still alive, but seriously ill (in a touching letter to Kay Boyle, Carnevali writes: "a great man, Robert MacAlmon, came to see me here . . . took all my writings with him, and he will perhaps make a book out of them!" [qtd. in Ford 54]). In his essay on Carnevali, William Boelhower notes that "there is (there cannot be) no definitive version of . . . *The First God*, the two available are both approximations." Significantly, he goes on to observe that the question of textual accuracy is "ultimately beside the point, for, at the aesthetic level of form . . . it is obvious that the author was not able to complete his autobiography" (*Immigrant* 140). Indeed, it seems to me that any kind of caution or reservation about the "reliability" of Carnevali's published works virtually evaporates from one's mind when one actually reads the texts, in any version. Then it cannot but be acknowledged that the voice we are hearing is a powerful and eloquent one that it is, in fact, like nobody else's.

Based as it is on a series of sensory impressions and a color pattern, Carnevali's evocation of the earliest and remotest phases of his life suggestively mimics the way our memory works, piecing together mental fragments. The colors white, pink, and black point to and, as it were, sum up in a single sensation, the periods of his childhood, his school years, and his first encounter with the New World. Carnevali's very first memory is that of a light-bathed interior with two female figures: "I remember a white room with white sunlight coming in from tall windows: in it my mother and an old lady, a very white old lady, stooping attentively over me, I may have been from two to three years old" ("God" 74). From that moment on there is a perceptible movement from light to dark, a massing of clouds over the external and inner landscapes of his life. No sooner have we read the above passage, than the sense of the frailty of life, of the impending presence of death, begins to pervade the text. Carnevali's recollection of scenes from his childhood is in fact interspersed with an impressive and disquieting series of episodes in which either his own life or that of the people who gravitate around him nearly comes to an untimely end. Even when the setting of his memories is at its most idyllic, as in his descriptions of the Tuscan and Piedmontese countryside, the impression is that death is constantly lying in wait.

When death eventually does strike, it carries away the two most important women in Carnevali's life, his mother and his aunt Melania (whose life story is narrated in "Tale One" of *A Hurried Man*, 11-23). As Carnevali moves on to tell of the time when he went to live with his father (at the age of eleven) and of his experience in three boarding schools, we pass to a male-dominated landscape, one in which the darkness clearly prevails over the light. Indeed, in the striking portrayal that the author draws of his father,[4] darkness seems almost to take on a human shape.

> My father is a tall man, almost six feet tall, who carries around a dark face and hides a dark heart . . . My father had a most vicious laugh: he showed his teeth when he laughed, which gave him the aspect of a ferocious beast . . . when [his laugh] was vented upon one of his little children it was like a snake running over a white plate. (*Autobiography* 40-42)

Here it is as if Carnevali were reproducing a very early impression. There is something vaguely exaggerated in the father's proportions and features – suggesting a cross between an ogre and the bogey-man – which is characteristic of a threatening adult figure as seen from the point of view of a very young person. The description seems to condense all memories of childhood fears and nightmares. The father's presence casts a literal shadow over the household, depriving it of light and warmth. In a startling reworking of one of the most typical images of parental tenderness – a father reading aloud to his children – Emanuel goes as far as to attribute a blasphemous, demoniacal quality to his father's voice: "he reads so coldly that I fear for my soul when I hear him" (*Autobiography* 40).

The impossibility of living with an individual qualified as "the most ignoble of men" ("God" 76), with a parent turned "archenemy," is the principal motive behind Carnevali's decision to leave Italy for the United States. What precipitates the crisis between father and son is Carnevali's expulsion from a Venice boarding school following the discovery of his infatuation with a fellow student.[5] Carnevali calls this section of the narrative "pink," because "in comparison with parts to come it is surely meek and mild" (*Autobiography* 44). Its dominant motif, however, is a sense of claustrophobia and an intolerance of discipline that anticipate the atmosphere of the hospitals and sanatoriums in the final part of the book.

Expelled from Venice,[6] the city to take "one look" at which – he writes – he would have given away "all modernity" (*Autobiography* 54), Carnevali finds refuge in the very heart of modernity, in the epitome of newness: New York. He passes from a city of silence to one of continuous din, from stillness to incessant motion, from the airy grace of lace-like palaces to an "awful network of fire escapes" (*Autobiography* 54 and 73). The change of scene could hardly have been more radical, more traumatic. Carnevali never really explains why he chose the United States rather than another country for his new life, as if there were no need to, as if the very distance, and difference, between Italy and the United States were the obvious reason for his choice. For where could a young man who had repudiated his father go if not to a nation that was, by definition, "young" and whose very birth had originated from a violent rebellion against its fatherland? Here was a country where, in Carnevali's words, "one could be young without feeling ashamed about it" (*America* 92), a country that was "tired of the Family," that damned "the European shackles of the Family" [*Autobiography* 160]).

In New York this man who defined himself "a running thing, a hurried man" (*Autobiography* 148), is outrun by the rhythm of the city and hence forced to launch himself into an endless and anxious chase after life. One notices a new urgency in Carnevali's writing in this section of the narrative, almost a propulsive quality in his sentences that effectively captures the tempo of the New York scene. Exemplary in this sense is a passage describing the author's entrance in the labor force of the metropolis:

> The JOB, that damnable affair, THE JOB. Nightmare of the hunted, THE JOB, this misery, this anxiety, this kind of neurasthenia, this ungrateful, this blood-sucking thing. THE JOB, this piecemeal death, this fear that grips you in the stomach, this sovereign lady who leaks terror, who eats the very heart out of man . . . My job was love and terror to me; thoughts of it kept me awake at night. For four days I had almost starved in that room in Twelfth Street and to think of losing my job was disaster and despair. I gave myself enthusiastically to it, working like a horse, and at night dreaming of the piles and stacks of dishes, dishes, dishes. (*Autobiography* 76-77)

In many ways Carnevali's American adventure follows the trajectory of the typical immigrant experience, but at record speed. Poverty, hunger, the despondent walks in the streets of New York, the menial jobs, the implausible schemes to make money, are all part of his experience – what is striking is the acceleration in the succession of these well-known phases.

It is interesting that one of Carnevali's failed attempts at making a living consists in writing "scenarios for the movies" (*Autobiography* 94 – unfortunately all his scripts were rejected), for the description of his life, of the days spent doing countless different jobs, of the nights spent in sordid furnished rooms, has something of the hurried and jerky pace of early motion pictures. It is also significant that the vehicle of his very first literary efforts turns out to be the latest and most modern form of expression (cinema), an art that, perhaps more than any other, may be aptly called the language of the New World:

> La, la, set it loose, shake your legs, run about like a fool, bring in the bloody roast beef, split the juice in the back and get the sack for it. Drop a piece of ice down a lady's bosom and go fishing for it. Oh, la, choke them with mayonnaise, stifle them under a wave of potage, yell "One soup, two soup and a bottle of champagne!" and to hell and damnation. Corks struggle in vain to attain joy. (*Autobiography* 90)

Recalling his beginnings as a poet Carnevali, as is the custom throughout the narrative, gives no dates and simply says: "and all of a sudden I began to write: rhymed poems at first, absurd, rhymed poetry which I sent to more than twenty magazines, getting nothing but rejection slips in return" (*Autobiography* 95). Even before encountering this statement, however, the reader of the New York section of the book cannot but become aware of the author's hyperactive gaze, of a way of looking at things that is characteristic of someone trying to absorb and transform the surrounding reality. To do the latter, however, ultimately proves impossible, as the metropolis imperturbably resists all his efforts. His aspiration to "impose his cosmic vision on the world" (Boelhower, *Immigrant* 168) remains unfulfilled. Rather, like the protagonist of Whitman's poem "There Was a Child Went Forth," Carnevali in New York and later in Chicago can become what he sees, but what he sees is immensurable, overflowing, dispersive, and restless. In a telling passage he refers to himself and his brother – recently arrived from Italy[7] and "rediscovered" by the author as fellow immigrant – as "two castaways on a raft in mid-ocean" (*Autobiography* 85). The image suggests Italian versions of Huck Finn and Jim, except that the river has been replaced by an immense and directionless ocean: the metropolis, a boundless field of signs. Like Twain's characters, the displaced Italian brothers may be seen as fugitives, homeless travelers in a hostile world. But whereas Huck's and Jim's journey down the Mississippi is also a journey toward identity, the "raft" evoked by Carnevali is drifting through the sea/city.

"Contaminated by the metropolis," to quote again from Boelhower, "the poet fails to find a totalizing form" (*Immigrant* 173), hence the sense of frustration and, at times, of enraged impotence that runs through the narrative. Even the references to what Carnevali calls the "golden period" of his life – his early literary successes, like the publication of his verses in the magazine *Poetry* – ultimately seem little more than isolated moments of superficial contentment. Significantly enough, in the Chicago section of the *Autobiography* the most promising phase of the author's literary career coincides with the beginning of his illness, with a descent into madness. In recreating and re-inventing his life in the narrative, Carnevali effaces all differences and barriers between life and art and makes them merge. Thus the actual, frighteningly "concrete" diseases he contracted in Chicago (syphilis, Spanish influenza, and encephalitis) lose nearly all physical connotations in the narrative and become a malady of the body, the mind, and the soul. It is tempting, then, to suggest that Carnevali loses his mind in the attempt to forge out of himself a poetic persona commensurate with the task of expressing American reality. He develops, in his words, an "appetite for madness," he becomes "the prey of neurotic obsessions which destroy the soul from within" (*Autobiography* 166 and 172) and finally gives vent to his delirious manifesto:

> I felt I belonged to the nineteenth century more than to any other, perhaps entirely, insanely, to the nineteenth century. The nineteenth century was made up of masks: the masks of poetry, Paul Verlaine, Arthur Rimbaud, Verhaeren, Carducci, Leopardi – all more or less crazy, all more or less sick; and Baudelaire altogether crazy... I believed absolutely now that I was the Only God... I cried out as loud as possible my crazy formula of godhead, repeating that I was for myself and for all men the First God, the Only God. (*Autobiography* 176)

As a result of outbursts such as this one Carnevali ends up in the Psychopathic Ward of Saint Luke's Hospital, Chicago (where, he says, he "made apostles" among the patients [*Autobiography* 181]) and from there, thanks to the financial help of his friends, moves to a private sanatorium for his convalescence. After being discharged, following the advice of his doctor, Carnevali spends what he calls "the last great beautiful days of my life" (*Autobiography* 191) on the shores of Lake Michigan and in the Minnesota woods. It is a fascinating wilderness episode, which at times reads like a deranged, hallucinated version of *Walden*. Living in rough shelters, swimming in the lake waters, lying on the sand dunes, eating wild berries, Carnevali seems to find temporary peace in a life reduced to the essentials of being ("my life was thus divided: I got up at sunrise and went straight into the water. Then I came back and cooked my inevitable oatmeal . . . then I would fall asleep swathed in sunlight" [*Autobiography* 192-3]). Yet his feel of the place, the sense of enjoyment and even exhilaration he experiences in the wilderness is never entirely free from disturbing signs of mental and emotional imbalance. Rapturous evocations of nature's colors, sounds, and odors are repeatedly upset by sudden disquieting images (an orchid looking "like a swollen face") or violent fits of depression ("there was no help for me, because of the major sin I had committed: that of loving success" [*Autobi-*

ography 193 and 194]), a sinister reminder of his unconquered illness.

There is no real transition between the end of the American part of the narrative and the concluding section, set in the little Italian town of Bazzano, near Bologna. The change of scene is rather abrupt: it is as if we suddenly woke up there, after a long and feverish dream. Instead of recounting his return voyage to Italy, Carnevali takes leave from America and salutes his native country with a poem whose rather humorous conclusion – "O Italy, O great shoe, do not/Kick me away again!" (201) – sets the tone for the last section of the book. Describing his life in a public hospital in Bazzano or in a private clinic in Bologna, the ailing Carnevali turns into a witty and pungent satirical observer. With their portrayals of doctors, patients, and visitors, the final pages of the *Autobiography* offer a remarkable gallery of grotesques.

It was in Bazzano that the editor of the *Autobiography*, Kay Boyle, met Carnevali and was profoundly affected both by his physical state and by his sensitivity (which was fitting as, at that stage, it must have been impossible to tell where the one ended and the other began). She felt she had found a kindred spirit, a kindred spirit trapped in a shaking body, and in a short while she found herself laughing and crying with him:

> On that bed there is the most beautiful man, shaking completely, all over, like a pinned butterfly. The whole bed seems in motion with his shaking – as if waves of water were breaking over and over and over and would never stop . . . I don't know why it is, you do not feel illness. You feel this endless agitation which will stop – you feel it has to stop. But he says it never stops – neither in the night. Never, Never. It never stops at all. (*Autobiography* 16-17)

Carnevali once referred to his condition as a "modern sickness" which made him "ridiculous, shattered and broken to smithereens" (*Autobiography* 124), thinking perhaps that there was a terrible and cruel irony in the fact that a "hurried man" should end his days mostly confined to bed and yet shaken by a perpetual motion. It was as if the violent tremor of his body was the ultimate form of that 20th-century restlessness and frenzy he had so tellingly incarnated in his life and writings.

THE ITALIAN AMERICAN MAN'S BURDEN

Masculinity in John Fante and Jerre Mangione

There was not much devotion to, not much love for learning and the written word among the Italians who reached America's shores with the great wave of immigration between 1880 and 1920. A large part of them had had little or no schooling and came from the rural south of Italy, where experience had taught them to be wary of those who were educated and could read and write. In their native land learning was almost invariably the accomplice of power and privilege in a social and economic system that had always cheated and famished them, and that had finally expelled them from their native land. This attitude persisted, and was reinforced, in the New World, where the American school system was suspected (not without reason) of erecting insurmountable barriers between parents and children, disrupting the unity of the family and alienating younger generations from their cultural heritage.

The purpose of this essay is to show how two major Italian American authors, John Fante and Jerre Mangione, emerged from this milieu. I have looked at the ways in which the acts of reading and writing in their works represent a form of protest against family authority and values, as well as a forceful assertion of independence. In particular, I have tried to show how, through their dedication to literature, Fante and Mangione subverted traditional conceptions of masculinity. Indeed, these writers chose to disregard the deeply ingrained notion that a "real" man was exclusively a man of action and that reading and writing were somehow unmanly or emasculating pursuits.

Peter F. Murphy has written that male power and sexuality may be experienced as a burden when men are expected to live up to "macho standards of performance" (4). I believe this is particularly true of Italian and Italian American culture where, traditionally, so much emphasis has been placed on the value of manliness. All males are equal but, according to popular wisdom, Italian males are more so. Until not long ago, for example, the conviction was still widespread in Italy that Northern European women flocked to the Adriatic coast in the summer in search of "real" men. And the images of Italian American men in popular culture (from Valentino to Rocky) encourage illusory expectations of an (artificial) masculinity: Italian Americans too have a tradition to defend and carry on.

As Helen Barolini has aptly reminded us, an old Italian saying defines words as "female" and deeds as "male" (*parole femmine, fatti maschi*).[1] Interpreting the saying, Barolini explains: "Words are for women, frivolous and volatile, a pastime in the marketplace," while deeds are for men who "engage in action which is concrete, real" (*Chiaroscuro* 148). According to the author of a late 19th-century study of Italian proverbs (Passarini 16-17), words are female because they have neither "authority nor strength," and one is much better advised to stick to deeds. The inescapable implication is that the man who favors the former over the latter somehow betrays his natural role and shows a detrimental propensity for levity, inconsistency, and weakness.

The saying was symptomatic of a culture in which the man was expected to act out his authority and virility both at home and at work, and where working with one's hands commanded more respect and trust than any kind of intellectual activity. The expression is rarely heard nowadays, but it is still remembered, and one can safely assume it was well known among the millions of Italians who transferred to the U. S. between 1880 and 1920. Among these were the families of John Fante and Jerre Mangione who came, respectively, from the regions of Abruzzo and Sicily. Fante was born in Colorado, in 1909, and began publishing his first stories in the 1930s. Several of his short pieces, and his first novel *Wait Until Spring, Bandini* (1938), are based on his childhood experiences in Colorado. His masterpiece, *Ask the Dust* (1939), and most of his other works were inspired by his vicissitudes as a struggling author and, later, as a well-paid but frustrated screenwriter in California. He died in 1983, a year after the publication of his last novel, *Dreams from Bunker Hill* (1982).[2] Jerre Mangione (whose real name was Gerlando) was born the same year as Fante, in Rochester, New York. *Mount Allegro*, his memoir of Italian American life from the 1920s to the 1940s, came out in 1943. It was followed by other autobiographical works in which Mangione described both his impressions of the land that had given birth to his parents (*Reunion in Sicily*, 1950, and *The World Around Danilo Dolci*, 1968) and his formative years as an Italian American aspiring writer (*An Ethnic at Large*, 1978). He also wrote, among other things, two novels, and a history of Roosevelt's Federal Writers' Project, *The Dream and the Deal* (1972). Mangione died in 1998.

In his 1977 novel *The Brotherhood of the Grape*, John Fante stages a fierce battle of wills and world-views between a middle-aged writer, Henry Molise, and his father Nick, a stonemason. Enfeebled by age and heavy drinking, but desiring more than anything "a wall to build" (114), Nick Molise expects his son to exchange his pen for a trowel and help him erect a stone smokehouse in the mountains. When Henry mentions a previous engagement – a contract with a publisher – the old man reacts with a mixture of incredulity and contempt, spitting out the word "book" as if it were something obscene: "'Book! You call that work?'" (34). From his point of view writing is simply not something a man does for a living, and his son might as well be speaking to a wall when he pleads: "All I know how to do is string one word after another, like beads" (43). In his frustration and impatience the protagonist happens to describe his craft with the kind of image that is least likely to appeal to, or impress, his father. For stringing beads is traditionally regarded as a "womanish" job and was in fact one in which many Italian American women were employed, in factories or at home. Moreover, the simile between words and beads cannot but call to mind the rosary and the image of Italian women silently reciting their prayers, thus drawing the writer into the sphere of femininity.

If in this and other works by Fante the father-figure refuses to acknowledge writing as the proper occupation for a man, in Jerre Mangione's memoirs the narrator is confronted early on in life with his family's deep mistrust of the written word. A recollection of Sicilian immigrant life in Rochester, *Mount Allegro* has been aptly called a "group-biography" (Boelhower, *Immigrant* 192) in which the narrator shares the stage with a large cast of relatives and friends. One of the major characters is Uncle Nino, the most educated member of the family, whose nocturnal writing is referred to uneasily by his relatives, and is enveloped in an aura of secrecy and disrepute.

> If the truth were known, Uncle Nino was a writer himself. No one had ever read anything he wrote and he never talked of it. My Aunt Giovanna . . . said that he wrote late at night when she was trying to sleep. She said he kept his writings locked in his safe along with his stock of jewelry . . . Like many respectable people, my relatives considered writing some kind of secret vice and never became openly curious about my uncle's literary life. (*Mount* 140)

The culture evoked by Mangione is one that values communal living and gregariousness, and where men are expected to hold center stage, to win the respect of their peers through what David Gilmore calls "involvement in the public arena of acts and deeds and visible, concrete accomplishments" (36). In such a context the acts of reading and writing are construed as selfish, unhealthy and unfruitful, suggesting a form of mental onanism.[3] Objectionable in an adult like Uncle Nino, a passionate involvement with the written word is seen as a cause of great alarm when displayed by a boy: "[My mother] had an ancient Sicilian prejudice against books," Mangione explains in *Mount Allegro* (213), and in the companion volume *An Ethnic at Large* he recalls:

> My fantasy life was well nourished by the piles of books I brought home from the public libraries, most of which I read clandestinely in the bathroom or under the bed since my mother believed that too much reading could drive a person insane. (*Ethnic* 14)

The specters of madness, illness, and abnormality are also apprehensively evoked in the Molise household in Fante's *Brotherhood of the Grape*. The hours that Henry, in his late teens, used to spend reading in his parents' kitchen were interpreted as symptoms of an altered state, or worse. And if his mother would strike a note of anxious concern when she attributed the redness of his eyes to the flu, his father's angry words hinted at something graver, a breach of loyalty, a betrayal:

> My old man, the son of a bitch, lurching home with a snoutful of vino, yelling turn off the lights, get to bed, what the hell's come over you, for books were a drug and my addiction was alarming and I was hardly his son at all anymore . . . He should see a doctor, my father said. Find out what's wrong . . . *Be a Man. You know what a man is? A man works. He sweats. He digs. He pounds. He builds.* (*Brotherhood* 61 [emphasis added])

What both enrages and bewilders Nick Molise is the distinct feeling that his oldest son is failing him, that he is acting in a way that renders him unrecognizable, unapproachable, "Other" from his own father. Significantly, the above episode is remembered by Henry, thirty years later, as he is resting on his mother's bed, snug in a "cradle in the mattress that measured the contours of my mother's body" (*Brotherhood* 60). What induces Henry's journey back in time is the "sweet, earthy" odor of Italian spices that his mother's hair has left on the pillow, turning it into a scented passage that connects the bedroom with the other classic maternal locus, the kitchen. In the past as in the present Fante's writer/hero is thus shown removed from his father, and comfortably inhabiting his mother's space, feeling at home in her dimension.

That the recognition of literature as one's calling implies a removal from traditional models of masculinity is also suggested by the prominence in both Fante and Mangione of male figures who embody alternative, unconventional, and surprising styles of conduct. Mangione's Uncle Nino, to whom I referred earlier, is a case in point. The most important male character in *Mount Allegro* next to the narrator's father, this man is in the eyes of several members of his community a "useless person" (*Mount* 291). Childless and economically dependent on his wife Giovanna, he is seen as incapable of meeting two essential requirements of masculinity: efficiency in reproduction and financial provision. According to the standards of his fellow Sicilian immigrants, he is not "good at being a man" (to use Michael Herzfeld's expression, 46). The one field in which Uncle Nino outshines all his male relatives and friends is storytelling. Though highly valued[4] and appreciated as a form of public entertainment (as opposed to the a-social nature of writing), storytelling is not an activity that can especially enhance his status as a man, in which he can "prove himself a man." However enjoyable or instructive, the end product of storytelling – the story – is too impalpable, too ephemeral, to be regarded as having a practical value. It is only in Mangione's prose that the inestimable worth of Uncle Nino's talent is given its due:

> All that my Uncle Nino needed was the suggestion of a story; he would fill in the details, the sequences, the climaxes, and might even give it a title of his own. He had once read an Italian translation of Shakespeare (he pronounced it 'Shakispiro') and had developed his own versions of the playwright's best-known classics, though he insisted they were Shakespeare's . . . Uncle Nino could dramatize a set of facts more effectively than any of my relatives . . . His most effective trick was to introduce a climax every few minutes, piling one on top of the other, and giving the impression all the while he told his story that each climax was the final one. He punctuated his stories with long, tantalizing pauses and a versatile set of facial expressions, which included a diabolically suggestive leer and the raising of either his left or right red-haired eyebrow. (*Mount* 139, 141)

What further renders Uncle Nino unlike other men is the fact that he does not inspire awe or reverence in children. Rather than as a figure of power and authority, they recognize him as a kindred spirit ("We treated him as one of us, letting him join in our games" *Mount* 137). His ever-active imagination and, in particular, his way with words, seem then to be associated with a gentle, boyish quality that distances him from the world of rough, domineering, and aggressive masculinity. The impression is confirmed by the poignant final tribute Mangione pays to Uncle Nino in the concluding section of *Mount Allegro*, which he added to the 1981 reissue of the book. Before relating the last days of the life of his uncle, Mangione declares that "whatever faults his contemporaries found in him did not diminish his appeal for all the children in our family . . . we felt more closely related to him than we did toward most of the other relatives" (291).

I find it intriguing that Nino is the only character in *Mount*

Allegro to actually use the words "feminine" and "masculine" (51), and he does so to describe, respectively, the Italian language and the Sicilian dialect. Mangione attributes this definition to a difference in sound between the two idioms, where the "softness" of Italian contrasts with the "harshness" of Sicilian. He also points out that even those Sicilians who could speak Italian rarely did so out of fear of sounding snobbish or affected. By contrast Uncle Nino is said to have delighted in speaking Italian on public occasions, such as large family gatherings or celebrations, further proof, I believe, of his remarkable nonconformism and independence.

In some of Fante's short stories the valorization of a non-traditional, non-exploitative, non-hierarchical model of relationship between men and women coincides with the crushing defeat of the representatives of machismo. Thus in the novella "A Wife for Dino Rossi" (1940) the meek, soft-spoken and gentle bachelor of the title imparts a meaningful lesson in decency and integrity to Guido Toscana, the loud, boastful, fearfully virile bricklayer who married the woman they both loved as young men. Throughout the story Fante makes it clear that Dino and Guido's wife, Maria, have a common language of courteousness, fairness and respect that goes beyond words and is as far removed as possible from Guido's Mussolini-like posturing.[5] In the end Guido's plan to marry Dino to an adventuress who had been his mistress fails miserably and it costs him the admiration and esteem of his oldest son. No punishment could be greater for a man who sees his male offspring as the living incarnation of his masculinity, and his claim to immortality: "My sons. Flesh of my flesh, bone of my bone. My handiwork . . . I created these boys, I, and I alone . . . When I am gone from this earth, my spirit goes on and on in the flesh of these boys, and their sons, and their sons' sons" (*Wine* 73).

In "A Nun No More" (1940), Fante tells the story of how

a young woman named Regina Toscana came to abandon her decision to become a nun – which she had strenuously defended against intense family pressure – and decided to marry a perfect stranger. The lucky man in question is significantly described as different from the other male characters in the story both in appearance (being a redhead, like Fante) and, most importantly, in his demeanor toward Regina. "He was an Italian," the narrator tells us, "but not of the ordinary kind" (*Wine* 183), the norm in Italian male behavior being represented by the men who gravitate around the heroine. These include her bossy, fierce-tempered brother Tony – who demands that she "forget about the nun business" (*Wine* 177) and marry a man of his choice – and the various suitors he shoves in her way. Regina, however, is adamant in her resolve to join the Church and valiantly resists the threats of her brother and the attentions of, among others, an uncouth grocer by the alarming name of Martello ("hammer"), and a gun-flashing gangster. The men who try to assert their authority by vulgarly displaying their brute force, wealth or power, achieve nothing beyond making fools of themselves. Then the unpretentious, likable hero makes his appearance (on a scaffold, in our case, since he is a construction worker) and unexpectedly triumphs by awakening the heroine's long-dormant capacity for amusement: he makes her laugh.[6]

At times an almost palpable sense of discomfort, of painful embarrassment, exudes from Fante's and Mangione's treatment of the male characters who typify aggressive and dominant masculinity. One feels that the example of tyrannical and/ or philandering fathers, husbands, and brothers is part of what they wanted to leave behind them when they departed from their homes and communities to become writers.

In Fante's greatest, and most deeply felt novel, *Ask the*

Dust, the author/hero bitterly muses on the famous Italian lovers of the past (such as Casanova) and on his utter incapacity to emulate them. But when he writes a story in which he re-fashions himself in the guise of a Valentino-like figure, using his craft to give form and substance to a fantasy of male domination, the result repels him:

> On paper I stalked her like a tiger and beat her to the earth and overpowered her with my invincible strength. It ended with her creeping after me in the sand, tears streaming from her eyes, beseeching me to have mercy upon her. Fine. Excellent. But when I read it over it was ugly and dull. I tore the pages and threw them away. (*Dust* 70)

In *Wait Until Spring, Bandini*, a father's need to assert his masculinity and vindicate his immigrant status by having an affair with an Anglo-American woman, brings his family to the verge of destruction. The devastating effects of his conduct are made frighteningly clear by the reaction of his oldest son Arturo, the center of consciousness in the story. Torn by irreconcilable loyalties, the boy wavers painfully between pride and anger, elation and despair:

> His father was a lowdown dog and all those things, but he was in that cottage now, and it certainly proved something. You couldn't be very lowdown if you could move in on something like that. You're quite a guy, Papa. You're killing Mamma, but you're wonderful. You and me both. Because some day I'll be doing it too . . . To think that he had come up here to bring his father home! How crazy he had been. Not for anything would he ever disturb the picture of his father in the splendor of that new world. His mother would have to suffer; he and his brother would have to go hungry. But it was worth it . . . As he hurried down the hill, skipping, sometimes tossing a stone into the ravine, his mind fed itself voraciously upon the scene he had just left. But one look at the wasted, sunken face of his mother sleeping the sleep that brought no rest, and he hated his father again. (*Bandini* 236-38)

In Mangione's *Mount Allegro* a conspicuous and embarrassed absence of authorial comment frames the telling of a story of avenged family honor in Sicily. In a sharp departure from the tone of amused participation that colors most of the stories recreated in the book, Mangione here simply relates the bare facts: "My father told how in Sicily his friend Carmelo Primavera became a hero for killing a man who had dealt lightly with his sister's honor" (*Mount* 192). Interestingly enough, the story centers on the clash between a man who is too free with words (the victim) and one who relies on deeds to speak for him (the killer). The victim ultimately pays with his life for something he has said, not to Carmelo's sister, but to Carmelo himself, having had the "effrontery" to call him brother-in-law. And Carmelo is hailed as a hero by his townspeople, to the point that the authorities are forced to release him from jail, precisely because he has acted "as a man." Throughout the story Mangione does not pass any judgment. Far more accurately than any comment, the author's silence measures the distance that separates him from his background on the question of what it means to be a man, an honorable man.

Even more disturbing than the events of this remote story was the rise of fascism in Italy, and its popularity among Italian American circles in the 1920s and 1930s. In the final part of *Mount Allegro* Mangione recalls how he used to listen in dismay to the pro-fascist talk of older Italian immigrants in New York's Washington Square. And when he traveled to Sicily, in 1936, he was shocked to discover how deeply fascist propaganda had sunk into the minds of the people. Mangione's strong and unfaltering anti-fascist stand is relevant here because it implies a rejection of that cult of virility which constituted such an essential part of the fascist ideology:

> Ethiopia had just been won and every loyal fascist felt like a Caesar holding the world by the tail. 'Soon,' a young law student declaimed to me, 'we're going to show the world that the French are an effeminate race who can't fight and

the English a weak and treacherous nation always trying to betray Italy. (*Mount* 254)

I opened this essay by quoting the proverbial definition of words as "female," an adjective patriarchal culture has traditionally used as synonymous with frivolous and undependable. I wish to go back to that saying here, for I believe a careful reading of Fante's and Mangione's writings can suggest an alternative interpretation: that women have a natural affinity with words, that they have a gift for narration (Scheherazade comes to mind), and that the men who are willing to listen to them can learn a great deal. It is a measure of Fante's and Mangione's willingness to listen and learn that they both paid significant homage to the women storytellers in their families. In *Mount Allegro* Mangione lovingly reproduces the elaborate description of a Sicilian religious festival by his Aunt Giovanna, acknowledging her uncommon power of observation and love for details. Moreover, at some point in the memoir he reveals that he "caught some of her love for playing with the word 'if'" (118), the key essential to setting in motion any narrative.

In Fante's stories "The Odyssey of a Wop" (1933) and "A Nun No More" the boy narrator (who is Fante's alter-ego) receives a valuable gift from his grandmother: his family's past in the form of a folktale. And in "A Kidnaping in the Family" (1936) the young protagonist and his mother collaborate in the reinvention of the events that led to her marriage with Guido Toscana, transforming his buffoonish declaration of love into a dashing outlaw's fearless exploit. Guido's drunken singing in a street of the Italian section of Denver is thus replaced by a romantic grand entrance on horseback:

"Yes!" she said. "He did kidnap me! He came one night when I was asleep and took me away."

"Yes!" I said "Yes!"
"He took me to an outlaw cabin in the mountains!"
"Sure! And he was carrying a gun, wasn't he?"
"Yes! a big gun! With a pearl handle."
"And he was riding a black horse."
"Oh," she said, "I shall never forget that horse. He was a beauty!"
"I just wanted to know," I said. "How long did he keep you prisoner?"
"Three days and nights."
"And on the third night he proposed to you, didn't he?"
Her eyes closed reminiscently.
"I shall never forget it," she said. "He got down on his knees and begged me to marry him."
"You wouldn't marry him at first, would you?"
"Not at first. I should say not! It was a long time before I said yes."
"But finally you did, huh?"
"Yes," she said. "Finally." (*Wine* 19-20)

Though in different ways, the autobiographical element is prominent in both Fante's and Mangione's works and is what, in a sense, truly sanctions their decision to become writers. For these two Italian American authors saved the world of their parents and grandparents from oblivion by using the very instrument – the written word – that was so little valued by their elders. In doing so they spurned the notion that a man can only rely on deeds to prove himself and leave behind him a worthy legacy. Fante and Mangione put their trust entirely in words, and no choice could have been wiser.

A DISSENTER'S RETURN

John Fante's Novel for the 1980s

In the same years – the early 1980s – in which Hollywood, as it were, arrived at the White House in the person of former actor Ronald Reagan, John Fante returned to novel-writing with *Dreams from Bunker Hill* (1982), a recreation of the Hollywood and Los Angeles of the mid-1830s. One cannot but admire the writer's perfect timing and, even more, the extraordinary affirmation of a commitment to art and life that this book represents. Fante was practically an invalid at the time he was working on *Dreams*, having lost his eyesight and both legs as a consequence of diabetes, but he managed to write the novel by dictating it to his wife. And it is not illness, depression, or fatigue that the book communicates, but rather vitality, rebelliousness, and irony. Indeed, if Fante's name were not on the cover, most readers might have thought a fresh new talent had burst upon the literary scene. If there is anything in the book that suggests Fante's age (he was in his early seventies when he wrote it), it is the assurance of his tone and the elegant smoothness of his style.

The publication of *Dreams* coincided with a revival of interest in Fante's early works (thanks, in part, to Charles Bukowski's sponsoring) and it is as if this long-overdue recognition had rejuvenated the ailing writer. For *Dreams* is anything but a remnant from a distant epoch in American writing. The book certainly covers familiar ground, adding as it does a fourth installment to the so-called "Arturo Bandini saga" – the story of an Italian American aspiring writer who appears as the hero of the novels *Wait Until Spring, Bandini* (1938), *The Road to Los Angeles* (written 1935-36, posthumously published in 1985), and *Ask the Dust* (1939). Yet even readers well acquainted with these three works, with their setting and characters, will find in *Dreams* a new urgency informing Fante's writing, as well as a more unconventional, episodic form, and a more marked taste for the grotesque.

The novel tells of the defeat of the aspiring author Arturo Bandini who, not unlike many of his real-life counterparts (the names of Faulkner, Fitzgerald, and Nathaniel West come to mind), is almost destroyed by his experience as a screenwriter in the "Dream Factory." The nature of this experience, it must be said, is somewhat elusive, in the sense that, unlike Fante, who did work on a number of films between 1935 and 1966, Bandini always remains a "virtual" screenwriter. All he writes, in fact, is a treatment for a film adaptation of Dreiser's *The Genius*, which remains unused (the project having been abandoned), and a script for a western entitled *Sin City*, from which he eventually withdraws his name in disgust after discovering that his initial version has been brutally altered. When *Sin City* is released Bandini goes to see it and is bitterly amused at finding that only two lines of his original dialogue have been retained, "Whoa!" and "Giddyup!," two lines that, as he says, testify to, and sum up, his "fulfillment as a screenwriter" (*Dreams* 127). His presence and role in the creative process that gives birth to a film have been canceled and it is as if he had never existed as a screenwriter. The absence of his name from the film credits and the almost total elimination of his words from the script convey something central to Fante's concerns in the novel. For the whole story can be said to be about the difficulty of leaving a mark, of "inscribing" one's name and presence onto the Los Angeles and Hollywood reality. Like a gigantic rubber wall, that reality stolidly resists any attempt to alter its placid, spongy, elastic surface – it always bounces back to its original condition, showing no visible sign of change. As Bandini comes to realize, one can become part of it, by letting oneself be absorbed by it, sucked into its smothering embrace, but only through a surrendering and dissolution of one's individuality. Conformity to the norm, this is what – to use Ezra Pound's expression – "the age demanded" (98-99), the age here referring perhaps as much to Fante's 1980s as to Bandini's 1930s. And this is precisely what the novel challenges and rejects, what it identifies as the target of its dissent.

In trying to assert himself, to defend his identity and vocation as a writer in downtown Los Angeles, the Colorado-born Arturo Bandini faces an uphill battle from the start. Significantly, as he describes the place where he lives and works in the first paragraph, he gives us a set of geographical coordinates ("a world bounded on the west by Bunker Hill, on the east by Los Angeles Street, on the south by Pershing Square, and on the north by Civic Center" [*Dreams* 9]). Despite the light-hearted tone of the narration, one senses a note of anxiety here, and the impression is that of an attempt to counteract the quality of placelessness and limitlessness of the scene, an attempt to claim and define one's space in a territory that, desert-like, cancels all signs and reference points.

At first the young Bandini seems willing to embrace a culture in which everyone has to sacrifice his or her individuality in order to play a predetermined role: the glamorous star, the successful producer, the brilliant director, etc. Having introduced himself to the reader as a promising young writer, fresh from the publication of his first story and, seemingly, on the way to becoming the protagonist of a rags-to-riches scenario, Bandini decides to invest his first cheque for his writing in a new wardrobe. His wallet being considerably less capacious than his ambitions and fantasies, he has to settle for a Goodwill store and second-hand clothes, but this does not diminish in the least the pleasure he takes in trying on a good suit and a pair of durable-looking shoes and admiring his new image in a mirror. As Fante describes the scene, it is as if his hero were trying on costumes and getting ready to walk onto a film set: "I bought . . . an irresistible glorious fedora. I set it jauntily at the side of my head" (*Dreams* 10). Such is the author's emphasis on the artificial, prop-like quality of the articles of clothing purchased by Bandini that, as he walks out of the store, one half expects the man and his outfit to dissociate and go their own separate ways. What actually happens, however, – as is natural in a place where clothes do make the man (and the woman) – is that the origin and quality of Bandini's apparel are quickly and effortlessly identified and exposed for what they are: "I walked out of the Goodwill and up Third Street, a new man. My boss, Abe Marx, was standing in front of the deli, as I approached. 'Good God, Bandini!' he exclaimed. 'You've been to the Goodwill or something?'" (*Dreams* 10). A few pages later, however, he is once again the "great Bandini," the talk of the town, the author of a story that the great man of American letters Heinrich Muller (standing for H. L. Mencken) has deemed worthy of being published in his magazine *The American Phoenix* (standing for *The American Mercury*). In his fine Goodwill pinstripe suit and his "rakish fedora," and a copy of *The American Phoenix* under his arm, Bandini seems carried away by the pure ecstasy of being alive:

> Down Olive Street I marched on the clear Sunday morning. The city seemed deserted, the street was quiet. I paused and listened. I heard something . It was the sound of happiness. It was my own heart beating softly, rhythmically. A clock, that's what it was, a little happiness machine. (*Dreams* 23)

Bandini is playing the distinguished gentleman – ("I crossed Fifth Street to the Biltmore Hotel. Well-dressed folk moved in and out through the revolving door. They were people like myself, neatly attired, the better class." [*Dreams* 23]) – and, as he talks to the Biltmore Hotel doorman and they both enjoy their ritual exchange of commonplace remarks, Fante fully renders the scene's air of comic unreality.

Compared to the kinds of deception that, as Fante shows in the course of the novel, are not only a common practice, but constitute the very essence of the Hollywood world, Bandini's "impersonations" appear as a rather innocuous form of daydreaming. Clearly they fool no one but himself and brand him unfailingly as the naive outsider. His tendency toward self-delusion mostly manifests itself in his ideas about fame, success, and women (as when, after dreaming of having a love affair with a beautiful stripper, he ends up in the arms of middle-aged Mrs Brownell, his landlady) but never, significantly, in anything to do with his craft. When it comes to writing, to the amount of effort, imagination, concentration and skill that goes into it, Bandini becomes deadly serious and finds himself at odds with the world surrounding him. One might say that for Bandini writing is something sacred (possibly the only sacred thing in his life), that it is a form of worship (with his mentor Heinrich Muller functioning very much like a God figure) far more deeply felt than his official creed, Catholicism. But in the course of his principal working experiences in Los Angeles – as editor for a literary agent and later as screenwriter – Bandini finds himself in environments in which writing is either debased or reduced to a form of prostitution. Quite fittingly, an atmosphere of profanation envelops both experiences, while the tone in which situations, places and people are described wavers between the grotesque and the nightmarish. The day Bandini walks into the office of literary agent Gustave Du Mont the impression is that the beastly, nauseating nature of his new job – editor of rotten manuscripts – is not merely anticipated by what confronts him, but is somehow made sensually palpable:

> The reception room lurched like an earthquake. I caught my breath and looked around. The place was full of cats. Cats on the chairs, on the valances, on the typewriter. Cats on the bookcases, in the bookcases. The stench was overpowering. The cats came to their feet and swirled around me, pressing my legs, rolling playfully over my shoes. On the floor and on the surface of the furniture a film of cat fur heaved and eddied like a pool of water. I crossed to an open window and looked down the fire escape. Cats were ascending and descending. A huge gray creature climbed toward me, the head of a salmon in his mouth. He brushed past me and leaped into the room. By now the whir of cat fur enveloped the air. (*Dreams* 11)

According to his boss, the job Bandini has been assigned is unpleasant but fairly easy. Most importantly, in the words of the former, "there is money in it if [one has got] the stomach" (12), this being apparently the only prerequisite for the position of editor. Similarly, when Bandini is offered the chance to work as a screenwriter for a big Hollywood studio, his hesitations – due to a self-confessed lack of experience – are met with somewhat disconcerting reassurances such as "that's fine" or "nothing to it" (42). Both episodes bespeak a culture in which the acts of reading, writing, of working with words, are regarded, presented, and "sold" as something facile, painless, and mechanical. To this Fante opposes his own relationship with literature, one in which the word is experienced as a living thing and its creation or fruition as an emotionally and physically demanding process. *Dreams* is perhaps at its most autobiographical when its hero recalls his first impact with literature in a library in Boulder, Colorado:

> One day I went to the bookshelves, and pulled out a book. It was *Winesburg, Ohio*. I sat at a long mahogany table and began to read. All at once my world turned over. The sky fell in. The book held me. The tears came. My heart beat fast. I read until my eyes burned. I took the book home. I read another Anderson. I read and I read, and I was heartsick and lonely and in love with a book, many books, until it came naturally, and I sat there with a pencil and a long tablet, and

> tried to write, until I felt I could not go on because the words would not come as they did in Anderson, they only came like drops of blood from my heart. (*Dreams* 57)

The narrator's words here are strongly reminiscent of those of the author in his correspondence with long-time friend and fellow writer Carey McWilliams. In a letter of 1936 Fante indicated "blood and pain" as the main ingredients of his novel *The Road to Los Angeles* and almost forty years later, in 1972, referred to *Ask to Dust* as "a painful boil [which] had to be bled and cleansed" (*Letters* 129, 294).

In *Dreams* Fante's love of, and reverence for, language also finds expression at the formal level. It can be recognized in his playful use of whimsical names (Gustave Du Mont, Velda van der Zee, The Duke of Sardinia), in the comically exaggerated manner in which he describes his hero's sexual life (these two elements are reminiscent of Thomas Pynchon's 1966 *The Crying of Lot 49*), and most of all in the musical quality of his prose. One feels the book ought to be read aloud and it is tempting to wonder whether this might be due, at least in part, to the fact that, as I mentioned earlier, the book was written by dictation, that it was "recited," as it were, and then transcribed.

It is definitely not love of writing, nor suffering, nor any other lacerating passion that Fante's Hollywood requires from its writers. The industry calls for standardized emotions and messages, for a travesty of moral values that is just as fake as the pastiche of architectural styles of the stars' mansions. As Fante sees it, in such an environment it is not possible to preserve the integrity of one's own, unique consciousness or, for that matter, of one's conscience. Deprived of that which forms their individuality, of that which differentiates them, even talented writers become part of an amorphous mass:

> My assignment from Harry Schindler was an unfathomable mystery. I spent the days reading his screenplays, a dozen of them, one a day, none of which I cared for. He was a specialist in gangster films and if you looked closely you discovered that all his scripts were essentially the same, the same plot,

the same characters, the same morality. I read them and set them aside. Sometimes I left the office and wandered down the halls. On each office door I saw the nameplate of the famous – Ben Hecht, Tess Slessinger, Dalton Trumbo, Nat West, Horace McCoy, Abem Candel, Frank Edgington. Sometimes I saw these writers entering or leaving their offices. They all looked alike to me. I didn't know them, and they didn't know me. (*Dreams* 45)

After two weeks at the studio Bandini realizes that he is being generously paid for doing nothing and his desperate request for "something to write" is dismissed with rather surreal expressions such as "You're doing a great job" and "Keep up the good work" (*Dreams* 48). But neither these words nor his impressive pay-cheque can assuage his mounting sense of uneasiness ("I didn't want charity. I wanted to be brilliant on paper, to turn fine phrases" [*Dreams* 48]), his fear of joining the ranks of his famous colleagues, of becoming a mere nameplate on an office door. It is as if Hollywood had the power of disembodying people ("it was as if [my boss] did not see me at all as he walked by" [*Dreams* 71]), of turning them into labels. This idea also emerges in Fante's portrayal of Velda van der Zee, an experienced screenwriter with whom Bandini is supposed to collaborate on the script of the film *Sin City*. A walking, grotesque mask of heavy make-up, this woman is never shown in the act of writing. In fact, all she does during her sessions with Bandini is to shower her young colleague with a cascade of famous names:

> Words tumbled from her lips, unstoppable. No doubt about it, she was a dingbat. She lived in a world of names, not bodies, not human beings, but famous names. Nothing she said could possibly be true. She simply invented as she prattled on. She was a liar, a lovable liar, her mind bubbling with preposterous tales. (*Dreams* 81)

Wishing to escape from this world of names, Bandini breaks ties with Hollywood and moves to Terminal Island, a strip of white sand in the Los Angeles harbor, mostly inhabited by

Filipino and Japanese immigrants. Earlier in the novel, at the height of his non-writing Hollywood career, he had confessed to a friend that he was powerfully drawn to Terminal Island, that he liked to picture himself in one of the beach houses, sitting alone in front of his typewriter, that he thought the place was beautiful and that it gave him "a warm feeling" (*Dreams* 48). For all his enthusiasm for this "paradise" (101), however, Bandini cannot quite bridge the distance that separates him from the place and its inhabitants, he cannot quite identify with them. As signaled by his use of the word "picturesque" (47) and his description of the gestures and manners of his Japanese landlady (102), his gaze never ceases to be that of the sympathetic visitor, a gaze which is incapable of going beyond externals. This distance is also due, at least in part, to Bandini's own insecurities as a member of an ethnic minority, insecurities that, as Stephen Cooper has justly pointed out, seem to take on a human shape in the character of Bandini's next-door neighbor, an Italian American wrestler called "The Duke of Sardinia." Significantly enough, it is this "veriest caricature of the Italian ethnic, all accent and onion and garlic" ("Eternal" 94) that ultimately pushes Bandini away from Terminal Island.

This expulsion from paradise places Bandini on a frustrating and painful road that leads him first to his old hotel in Bunker Hill, where his landlady and former lover refuses to take him back, and then to his home place Boulder, Colorado. But even here, in spite of the warm welcome he receives from his family, he cannot remain for long. At a party he alienates his acquaintances by boasting of all the famous Hollywood people he has supposedly met and then, disgusted as much with himself as with his listeners, he abruptly decides to return to Southern California. The scene is worth noticing for the way in which Fante makes us sense distinctly the pernicious lingering effects of his hero's Hollywood experience. His name-dropping at the party sounds startlingly similar to that of Velda van der Zee: it is as if he had been contaminated by her, as if he had turned, temporarily, into her replica.

The search for a place – for a space – in which to claim and express one's real self becomes at this point urgent, if not frantic. But like his homecoming, his new return to Bunker Hill proves painfully disappointing (during his absence Mrs Brownell has died of a stroke). One is reminded here of a phrase Nathaniel Hawthorne used in *The Marble Faun* (1860) to warn travelers of the dismaying consequences that residence in a foreign country might produce. Upon their return, travelers may discover that they no longer belong, that "life has shifted its reality to the spot where we deemed ourselves only temporary residents" (461) and that, as a result, one is left without any place he or she can call home. Granted the difference in time, place, and situation, I believe Hawthorne's reflections may apply to Fante's novel where, indeed, Bandini's native Colorado and Southern California are as distant and unrelated as two different countries.

In the end the only place that welcomes, so to speak, Arturo Bandini is a cheap, dirty, bare room on Temple street, Los Angeles, above a Filipino restaurant, the "smallest, most uninviting room" (*Dreams* 146) in town, where he had already stayed briefly, prior to his return visit to Boulder. Squalid though the place certainly looks (the antithesis of glamorous Hollywood), it does contain an object of inestimable value: Bandini's typewriter.

> [the manager] stood in the doorway holding my portable typewriter. It startled me, not because it was there, but because I had completely forgotten it. He placed it on the table and I thanked him. Closing the door, I opened a suitcase and took out a copy of Knut Hamsun's *Hunger*. It was a treasured piece, constantly with me since the day I stole it from the Boulder library . . . I stretched out on the bed and slept. It

> was twilight when I awakened and turned on the light. I felt better, no longer tired. I went to the typewriter and sat before it. My thought was to write a sentence, a single perfect sentence. If I could write one good sentence I could write two and if I could write two I could write three, and if I could write three I could write forever. But suppose I failed? Suppose I had lost all of my beautiful talent? . . . What would happen to me? . . . I had seventeen dollars in my wallet. Seventeen dollars and the fear of writing. I sat erect before the typewriter and blew on my fingers. Please God, please Knut Hamsun, don't desert me now. I started to write and I wrote:
>
> "The time has come," the Walrus said,
> "To talk of many things:
> Of shoes – and ships – and sealing wax –
> Of cabbages – and kings –"
> I looked at it and wet my lips. It wasn't mine, but what the hell, a man had to start someplace." (*Dreams* 146-47)

Ultimately, it is not so much in the room of the Filipino hotel, but on that sheet of paper, that Bandini finds his place. By borrowing a passage from a virtuoso of the written word – Lewis Carroll – by making it his own, he reaffirms his commitment to language and writing as well as his identity and role as an artist. There, on that piece of paper, he finds what Tony Tanner has called the "environment of freedom made possible by language" (20), the only "space" in Los Angeles where he can leave a mark, the field from which he can launch his challenge to the conditioning forces surrounding him. In "La poubelle agréée" Italo Calvino defined paper as the "tender daughter of the forests, [the] living space for the writing and reading man" (78).[1] So it proves for Arturo Bandini at the beginning of his life as a writer; so it proved for John Fante at the end of his.

"IN THE NAME OF THE FARTHER"

The Poetry of Pasquale Verdicchio

In criticism on North American authors of Italian background one often observes a regrettable tendency to think of the writers' identity as an arena, or a battleground, in which opposite forces vie for supremacy.[1] The Italian side, it is almost invariably assumed, is the weaker of the two, doomed to be ultimately defeated and conquered. Since the confrontation is staged on American soil, time is believed to be the American side's most powerful ally. Year after year, generation after generation, the Italianness of the Italian North American author is destined to lose strength, to become more and more diluted, until it is hardly recognizable. What remains of it will occasionally reemerge here and there, peeping out, as it were, in the form of place names or references to food, amid a sea of Americanness.

The scene of Italian North American writing, however, is far more complex and varied than this. It extends from the early travelers, adventurers, and missionaries of the 17th, 18th and 19th centuries, to the immigrants of the 1880-1920 period and those who followed in later years, and includes the current expatriates: students, academics, artists, who live and write in North America. Pasquale Verdicchio embodies this complex, multi-faceted character. His identity and his poetry defy simple, clear-cut categorizations. Born in Naples in 1954, he moved to Canada in the late sixties and since 1980 has been living in Southern California, where he teaches Italian literature and writing at the University of California, San Diego. He is the author of several collections of poetry, numerous essays (some of which have been collected in the recent volume *Devils in Paradise*), and has published translations of the works of, among others, Antonio Porta, Pier Paolo Pasolini, Giorgio Caproni, and Alda Merini. Reading his books of poems in succession, from *Moving Landscape* (1985) to his most recent effort *Approaches to Absence* (1994), one cannot but notice how the foreign, Italian, Neapolitan element in his verse, far from receding, has progressively gained prominence, affecting not so much his subject matter, as the verbal and syntactic texture of his writing. The longer he lives in North America, it would seem, the more hybrid he becomes.

Although Verdicchio's poetic trajectory is sometimes hard to map (which is fitting for one who identifies with the figure of the nomad, as he does), there is no doubt that he has been moving away from standard English usage and forms. His desire to "contaminate" English with other languages, as he put it in a recent essay (*Devils* 38), is much more visible in his recent poems than in his early ones. Indeed, in his first book *Moving Landscape* he seems intent, for the most part, on getting the most out of the aural resources of English alone, on releasing the "magic of the pure sound of words" (to use Jakobson's and Waugh's expression, 247). One recognizes this in his pronounced taste for alliteration, and his propensity for the rounded phoneme "w," which gives a lovely aerial quality to "Red-Winged Blackbird" (the poem that opens *Moving Landscape*). As they form the words "wind" and "wing," the lips open outwards, as if the words themselves were on the point of taking flight:

> Wind. Wind
> and wings of birds.
> A red-winged blackbird
> sparks against the sky
> and green shrubs;
> comes to rest in the safety

> of calls that break
> against our words,
> clear and intelligible words,
> and light the evening
> with the fire of meaning. (11)

The poet's passionate commitment to language is given form and substance in the text by the physical, tactile presence of "words." Words are "clean and intelligible," like a crystal or, given their inflammable nature, like a fragment of flint. In this and other poems of *Moving Landscape* the stuff words are made of suggests a hard, inorganic material, that needs to be scraped or shattered to produce meaning. In the poem "Letter," for example, we read of "Another place name fallen/to the page, its letters broken/to mean a thousand words" (12). Besides the concreteness, the tangibility of words, the image suggests a dissemination of signs, to be gathered and reassembled to form new words, as one would do with the pieces of a puzzle or a mosaic. We can also be reminded of a kaleidoscope, in which no pattern remains the same for long, for words are very much a part of the shifting scene, the moving landscape of the title.

At times the impression is that the landscape (and everything in it), is conceived of as an immense manuscript that needs to be deciphered. Everything is "text": the fish in the sea, the human body, the fossils of extinct animals, the remains of ancient civilizations. In such an environment it is small wonder that the poet's senses need to be constantly on the alert. For even a hyperactive gaze such as his could not do justice alone to a scene where sound can take on the properties of light and light those of sound, as in "Between the Desert."

> The sea. Not the sea.
> Music reaches out from towers:
> notes reflected in the eyes of women.
> Desires, already memories,
> encrusted with onyx and agate.
> A traveler arrives, misunderstands
> the redundance that fills his eyes:

>   always leaving, always returning,
>   he finds himself between the desert. (*Moving* 19)

Sound is also, constantly, the protagonist of Verdicchio's poetry at the textual level, as in that teasing opening line, with what might be a faint echo of Hamlet's famous question, or in the poem "Ritual," where sibilants hiss like the wind: "The curtain on his door whispers/its movement in the wind. His/hands reach high into branches,/spill silent into the air:/a conversation . . ." (*Moving* 28).

In an interview given a year after the publication of *Moving Landscape*, Verdicchio describes one of his central themes: the idea of the writer as traveler. "To write is to migrate, to be in constant movement" (*Devils* 135), says Verdicchio, and this assertion is convincingly supported by his evocation of the figure of Ulysses in the poem "Artaud and Nobody."

>   During his great voyage
>   he changed his name to reflect
>   the seas he had traveled,
>   names of his experience.
>   To everyone he came to be
>   known as what the one-eyed visionary
>   had called him: Nobody.
>   Nobody returned home
>   to find he had never been there
>   and his name, usurped by words,
>   found its way across centuries
>   becoming over and over the traveler:
>   man searching and finding himself
>   tied against songs of mermaids
>   and temptation . . . (*Moving* 34)

No less relevant are Verdicchio's references, in this and other poems, to Dante, a poet-voyager himself and one of the supreme creators of the myth of Odysseus.

Verdicchio's 1990 book *Nomadic Trajectory* could be seen as a poetic rendering of those theories of rootlessness and distance that, according to Arjun Appadurai, are needed to deal with "the world we live in now" (325). Literally placed at a distance from his first two worlds, Italy and Canada, the California-resident Verdicchio has felt an affinity for the rootlessness of the nomad and the idea of movement between places, rather than from or to places, associated with that figure. Living and working in a sort of neutral ground, Verdicchio himself embodies a condition of in-betweenness, of transition between languages and cultures that finds expression in his poetry and translations.

Comparing *Nomadic Trajectory* with *Moving Landscape*, one observes in the former a considerable increase in Latinate words and unorthodox syntactic forms, and an extremely frugal use of punctuation. The latter feature is especially worth noticing in that, in a way, it gives the act of reading itself a "nomadic quality." We proceed unfettered from line to line, with that peculiar sense of freedom we experience in the absence of a pre-established direction or destination.

As Rosi Braidotti has pointed out, "the nomadic traveler is uniquely bent upon the act of going, the passing through," and is a figure that is well attuned to the "transitional movement that marks our historical situation." To adopt the "nomadic garb" allows Verdicchio, and us as readers, to resist "assimilation or homologation into dominant ways of representing the self" (Braidotti). The attractiveness of an unpredictable, nomadic trajectory becomes all the more apparent if we consider under what pressure so-called ethnic writers are, to limit themselves to a pre-established set of themes and images in exchange for recognition from the dominant culture.

Disappointing those critics who expect the "hyphenated writer" (Italo-American, Chinese-American, etc.) to strew his or her text with "ethnic crumbs" (so that *they* can find the way), Verdicchio alludes to his origins and his "expatriate" status with admirable discretion and indirectness. As Emily

Dickinson would have put it: when Verdicchio tells his story, he tells it slant. Thus in "Branta Candensis" the change of scene, the passage from one land to another, from one language to another, is almost entirely devoid of realistic details.

> A mouth full of names before the leaving
>
>   people at the open border:
> nothing and nothing to fear.
>
> Come expecting never again the transparence
> the sweetness of discourse;
> not what it started out to be,
> understand opposition:
>
> Cut from past experience of
> secrets revealed to hands and eyes
> kept from fleeing with the view
>
> the horizontal window of music
>
> *When the geese flew overhead*
> *I could not help but think*
> *of what lay north.* (*Nomadic* 10)

In "Parthenope" a ontage of voices, languages and different stylistic registers suggestively mimics the multi-layered historical texture of Naples, and gives an unconventional, unsentimental character to this revisitation of the poet's native city.

> Gulf   sweeping arm to comprehend
>
> *from Capo Miseno to the tip of*
> *Punta Campanella, protected by the heights*
> *rising with the unmistakable outline of Vesuvius*
>
> citizen   recounting the stories of others
>
> A grid of dissimulation   the city impervious
> shell of fiction: transferring metonymical placement
>
> an identity claimed by so many places
> one city yet all possible cities   in fragments . . .
>   (*Nomadic* 12)

A few poems in *Nomadic Trajectory* are divided into numbered sections one may think of as successive "removes" in the nomad/poet's travel narrative. The journey motif is further emphasized by the titles of four poems – "Between the Desert," "Encampment," "Oasis," and "Within Landmarks" – which form a sequence bearing the same name as the entire collection. In these compositions one detects, in addition to the aforesaid division in chapters, a "laceration" in the middle of the page, a blank space separating two uneven, jagged columns of text (which can even be read "vertically," as lists of words). This unusual structure induces the reader to pause, to look first at one "pile" of words, than at the other, before choosing his or her course. We thus become one with Verdicchio's poetic persona and his concern that:

> the ignorance of points leads astray;   we
> choose   the paths assessing significance
> Movement takes place   and always always
> between before and after   Exile constant
> for the nomad   who has every   and no place
>   ("Between the Desert," *Nomadic* 33)

The poet's interest in the "question of language," an expression that may refer both to the history of Italian culture and to the current situation of post-emigrant writers such as himself, creates a link between *Nomadic Trajectory* and Verdicchio's 1993 book *The Posthumous Poet: A Suite for Pier Paolo Pasolini*. The Figure of Dante, evoked in the long, composite poem "The Arsonist" (which closes *Nomadic Trajectory*), is followed in the later collection by those of Pasolini and Gramsci, whom Verdicchio has repeatedly acknowledged as major influences on his work. Like Dante, both Pasolini and Gramsci reflected on the linguistic heterogeneity of their country, a problem that has followed Italian immigrants to North America and other parts of the world and that continues to be relevant in today's

Italy. The question of the interaction or superimposition of languages and cultures becomes visible on the pages of *The Posthumous Poet*, in the form of translated titles of Pasolini's works and quotes from Gramsci. So does Verdicchio's strategy to – in his words – infiltrate the structure and "ideology of the [English] language" with Italian elements (*Devils* 145). At the aural level these presences may be said to produce a ventriloquial effect: the sound of voices coming from elsewhere and joining that of the poet.

> Heretical Empiricism. Where the poet stands. As a result of his body it extends well beyond. Language of the spectrum of non-dominant forces. Dried blood of miracles liquefies yearly. Inhabit the curvature of the Earth. At a point of preliminary observation. Are they not narrative structures homologous to capitalism? The geography of ideology well defined; the role of the intellectual. Free indirect discourse.
>
> Overcome obstacles by force
> of love, do not knock them down, but loosen them
> like the action of water on soil.

"Every hegemonic relation is necessarily pedagogic." . . .
(*Posthumous* 49)

The Posthumous Poet begins in a prayer-like tone ("In the language of the mother/in the language of the son/offer us a simple past/in place of an uncertain present" 11) and ends with a section (entitled "The Crucifying Code") that suggests a dirge or a requiem. It is only here that the violent death of Pasolini is explicitly mentioned ("the body of the poet battered by murderers" 61), but the whole composition – which I think is meant to be read in one sitting – may be said to lead up to that line. Not only is the idea of death introduced since the very title, but scattered among the lines are terms like "assassins," "wounds," "lacerated," "murderous," "torture," and executioner," that flash images of suffering and the brutal suppression of life.

But posthumous, by definition, is what remains after death, what, in a way, preserves a dead person's voice. The posthumous poet is then the poet who has survived his own physical decease, whose body is now the text of his works, which we may continue to study and interpret.

Verdicchio's poetry is at its most abstract and cerebral in the poet's recent collection, *Approaches to Absence*, published in 1994. As in *Moving Landscape* and *Nomadic Trajectory*, Verdicchio is still very much concerned with place and movement, but these categories have been stripped of almost all familiar connotations. Indeed, everything is so far removed from common experience, that one can get heady from the rarefied air emanating from Verdicchio's lines. Interestingly enough, the book includes a revised version of a sequence of poems titled "A Critical Geography" that was originally published as a chapbook in 1990. What clearly emerges from a comparative analysis of the two versions is that Verdicchio's guiding principle in the revision has been one of subtraction. A considerable number of words, and sometimes whole lines, have simply disappeared in the later edition. One notices that it is mostly objects belonging to the sphere of quotidian experience that have vanished from the scene. "Tile roof," "bicycles," "casements," letters," "shoes," and "canvas," are only some of the casualties of Verdicchio's ruthless editing. It may very well be that this "distillation" of reality is one of the "approaches to absence" to which the book refers.

In another section called "Translatio" the space where one would expect to find words is occasionally occupied by straight lines, arrows, dots, and signs that look like vertical dashes. Here reading poetry is as much a visual as an auditory experience. In addition, one can think of these signs as yet another language (after English, Italian, and Latin) being added to the poet's rich repertoire. "Translatio" indicates the transfer of something (words, for example) or someone from one place to another, from one context to another. And what is most valuable to Verdicchio, once again, is the transition itself, rather than the points of departure and arrival. The process of translation is particularly liberating for expatriates, Verdicchio suggests, in that it empowers them to explore their duality or multiplicity, without having to identify entirely with a single culture.

> the condition of expatriates who must write mutely
> out of step   constant readjustment intrinsic
> and extrinsic to the act of writing
>
>   to fall in step out of step
> tangential provocation of linguistic expression
> an eye off to the side
> keeping acculturation under watch
>
> translation is not becoming
> but (di)versifying . . . (*Approaches* 57)

"My house of language," Verdicchio acknowledges later in the same poem, has "no walls" (60). It is perhaps a mobile home that is always on the move, and which has cruised through all the developments and experimentation of his craft. Sometimes his readers may find it difficult to keep up with its speed and its sudden, daring turns, but if they manage to hang on to it they may be carried along in a fascinating journey.

NOTES

Foreword

1 On the first Italian translations of Fante's works, see Martino Marazzi's *Misteri di Little Italy* (58-66).
2 Recent publications of note on Italian American writing include: *Adjusting Sites: New Essays in Italian American Studies*, ed. William Boelhower and Rocco Pallone (1999), Helen Barolini's *Chiaroscuro: Essays of Identity* (1999), Mary Jo Bona's *Claiming a Tradition: Italian American Women Writers* (1999), Fred Gardaphé's *Italian Signs, American Streets: The Evolution of Italian American Narrative* (1996), Martino Marazzi's *Misteri di Little Italy: Storie e testi della letteratura italoamericana* (2001), *Il sogno italo-americano. Realtà e immaginario dell'emigrazione negli Stati Uniti*, ed. Sebastiano Martelli (1998), and Anthony Tamburri's *A Semiotic of Ethnicity: In (Re)Cognition of the Italian American Writer* (1998).

Early Narratives by Italian Americans

1 "Second life" is the happy expression another 19th-century Italian expatriate, Antonio Gallenga (1810-1895), used to define his experiences in England and North America.
2 As early as 1862, writing to General George B. McClellan, Cesnola groundlessly calls himself an "American citizen." However, in a telling letter to Assistant Secretary of War P.N. Watson, written immediately after his dismissal from service on February 2, 1863, he complains: "I have no friends . . . I am a foreigner, and I am an innocent man . . . If officers who are fighting for *their* country have to be treated in a such a way the war will never end" (quoted in McFadden 35, 42 [emphasis added]).
3 Cesnola submitted his narrative, signed it and swore as to its veracity in front of John Rogers, Commissioner of Deeds, in New York City, on the 15th of February, 1865.
4 It is interesting to compare Cesnola's report with *The Adventures of a Prisoner of War* (1865), a memoir by a Texan officer of Italian descent by the formidable name of Decimus et Ultimus Barziza (1838-1882). In his narrative Barziza repeatedly complains about the coarseness and vulgarity of Union soldiers and stresses, in particular, the fact that "they do not hold that high regard and true esteem for womanly virtue that characterize the chivalrous Southerners" (68-69).

Ten months in Libby Prison

1 The text used for this book was originally published in the *Bulletin* of the United States Sanitary Commission (Philadelphia? March 1865).

Monaca o strega?

1. All quotations are from the 1999 reprint of *At the End of the Santa Fe Trail* (Albuquerque: University of New Mexico Press).
2. Consider, for example, the distinction between "Italians" and "Sicilians" in Rosa Cassettari's memoir *Rosa: The Life of An Italian Immigrant* (transcribed and edited by Marie Hall Ets).
3. As Marc Simmons points out in his Foreword to the 1999 reprint of *At the End of the Santa Fe Trail*, references to dates in Segale's journal are often inaccurate, including the entry in which she recorded Billy the Kid's death: September 8, 1882 (Billy died on July 14, 1881). Indeed, historical evidence shows that, of the three encounters Segale claims to have had with Billy, only the third one could have taken place, though not on the date indicated in the journal (May 16, 1881). Simmons justly notes, however, that Segale's entries "rather than day by day, are in fact summaries of weeks or even months, hastily written up whenever Sister Blandina at long intervals found precious time that could be turned to authorship. This meant that she was obliged to rely upon memory in the reconstruction of events and recalling of conversations" (xx-xxi). Simmons further suggests, reporting the opinion of Father J. Steele, S.J., that Segale's journal entries are to be seen as part of the prose genre known as "edifying letters" which had inspirational rather than strictly historical purposes. What I wish to emphasize, however, is that, whether partly fictional or not, Segale's portrayal of Billy the Kid is unmistakably sympathetic and casts him in the unexpected role of the product and sacrificial victim of a violent society.

A "Lost Soul" in America

1. The English translation is mine. *Voglio disturbare l'America* ("I want to disturb America," henceforth indicated as *America*), edited by Gabriel Cacho Millet, is a collection of letters Carnevali wrote (in Italian) to Benedetto Croce, Giovanni Papini, and Carlo Linati. Millet's introductory essay and notes constitute an invaluable source of information on Carnevali's biography and literary production, with particular attention to his ties with modern Italian literature.
2. For my quotes I have used both *The Autobiography of Emanuel Carnevali* (1967) and the chapters originally published as "The First God" in *Americans Abroad* (1932).
3. For a useful comparative analysis of the different versions of Carnevali's text, see Mario Gelormini's "Reconstructions of Emanuel Carnevali's *The First God*" (1992-93).
4. Not surprisingly, in her preface to *Il Primo Dio*, Maria Pia Carnevali refers uneasily to Emanuel's unflattering portrayal of their father and insists on the fictional character of the book (9-11).
5. Mario Gelormini's above-mentioned study contains, in an Appendix, a reproduction of the letters exchanged between Carnevali's father and the headmaster of the Foscarini Boarding School, Venice, prior to Emanuel's expulsion.
6. After leaving Venice, Carnevali lived in Bologna for two years, and this period of his life is covered by *The Autobiography*. However, his description of Venice and New York as antithetical urban realities suggests that what he called "The Great Jump – Italy, U.S.A." (*Autobiography* 69) referred in particular to the cultural distance separating those two cities.
7. In this section of the narrative Carnevali is deliberately altering the facts concerning his brother's arrival in America. The two brothers, in fact, left together for the United States in 1914.

The Italian American Man's Burden

1. The saying is attributed to Pope Clemens VII, ruler of the Roman Catholic Church between 1523 and 1534 (Passarini 16-17), but is probably much older. In her essay, Helen Barolini uses the words "feminine" and "masculine" to translate the Italian *femmine* and *maschi*, but I consider "female" and "male" to be more appropriate.
2. For anyone interested in Fante's life and work, Stephen Cooper's beautifully written *Full of Life: A Biography of John Fante* is essential reading.
3. In his study of Italian American Narrative *Italian Signs, American Streets*, Fred L. Gardaphé recalls how, in the Little Italy where he grew up, the "self-isolation that reading requires was rarely possible and was even considered a dangerous invitation to blindness and insanity" (1).
4. On the significance of oral culture for Italian Americans, see Fred Gardaphe's essay "From Oral Tradition to Written Word."
5. On the treatment of gender in this story see also my essay "Masculinity and Femininity in John Fante's 'A Wife for Dino Rossi'" (88-94).
6. The plot line of "A Nun No More" is reminiscent of a number of popular folktales in which the hero wins the princess's hand not thanks to feats of strength or bravery, but through the gift of laughter. On the presence of folktale motifs in Italian American literature see Gardaphé's "From Oral Tradition to Written Word" and *Italian Signs, American Streets* (24-54).

A Dissenter's Return

1. The translation is mine.

"In the Name of the Farther"

1. I chose the last line of Verdicchio's "Fact/Confession" (*Approaches* 17) for the title of this essay because it admirably sums up his poetics, his endless fascination with movement, and his eagerness to explore new forms and styles.

WORKS CITED

Amfitheatrof, Erik. *The Children of Columbus; An Informal History of the Italians in the NewWorld*. Boston: Little, Brown and Company, 1973.

Appadurai, Arjun. "Disjuncture and Difference in the Global Cultural Economy."*Colonial Discourse and Post-Colonial Theory*. Ed. Patrick Williams and Laura Chrisman. New York: Harvester Wheatsheaf, 1994. 324-339.

Barolini, Helen. *Chiaroscuro: Essays of Identity*. Madison: University of Wisconsin Press, 1999.

—. Introduction. *The Dream Book: An Anthology of Writings by Italian American Women*. New York: Schocken Books, 1987. 3-56.

Barziza, Decimus et Ultimus. *The Adventures of a Prisoner of War, 1863-1864*. Ed. R. Henderson Shuffler. Austin: University of Texas Press, 1964.

Boelhower, William, and Rocco Pallone, ed. *Adjusting Sites: New Essays in Italian American Studies*. New York: Forum Italicum, 1999.

—. *Immigrant Autobiography in the United States*. Verona: Essedue Edizioni, 1982.

Bona, Mary Jo. *Claiming a Tradition: Italian American Women Writers*. Carbondale: Southern Illinois University Press, 1999.

Braidotti, Rosi. "Figurations of Nomadism: Homelessness and Rootlessness in Contemporary Social and Political Theory." Acoma Conference. Bergamo, 22 Mar. 1997.

Buonomo, Leonardo. "Masculinity and Femininity in John Fante's 'A Wife for Dino Rossi.'" *John Fante: A Critical Gathering*. Ed. Stephen Cooper and David Fine. Cranbury, N.J.: Fairleigh Dickinson University Press, 1999. 88-94.

Calvino, Italo. "La poubelle agréée." *Romanzi e racconti*. Ed. Claudio Milanini, Mario Barenghi e Bruno Falcetto. Vol. 3. *I Meridiani*. Milano: Mondadori, 1994. 3 vols. 59-79.

Carnevali, Emanuel. *The Autobiography of Emanuel Carnevali*. Ed. Kay Boyle. New York: Horizon Press, 1967.

—. "The First God." *Americans Abroad*. Ed. Peter Neagoe. The Hague: Service Press, 1932. 73-82.

—. *A Hurried Man*. Paris: Contact Editions, 1925.

—. *Il Primo Dio*. Ed. and Trans. Maria Pia Carnevali. Milan: Adelphi, 1978.

—.*Voglio disturbare l'America*. Ed. Gabriel Cacho Millet. Milan: La Casa Usher, 1980.

Cesnola, Luigi Palma di. *Cyprus: Its Ancient Cities, Tombs, and Temples*. London: John Murray, 1877.

Cooper, Stephen. *Full of Life: A Biography of John Fante*. New York: North Point Press, 2000.

—. "John Fante's Eternal City." *Los Angeles in Fiction*. Ed. David Fine. Albuquerque: University of New Mexico Press, 1995. 83-99.

Craveri, Marcello. *Sante e streghe*. Milan: Feltrinelli, 1980.

Durante, Francesco, ed. *Italoamericana. Storia e letteratura degli italiani negli Stati Uniti 1776-1880*. Milano: Mondadori, 2001.

Eakin, Paul John. *Fictions in Autobiography; Studies in the Art of Self-Invention*. Princeton: Princeton University Press, 1985.
Ets, Marie Hall, comp. and ed. *Rosa: The Life of an Italian Immigrant*. Minneapolis: University of Minnesota Press, 1970.
Fante, John. *Ask the Dust*. 1939. Santa Rosa, Ca: Black Sparrow Press, 1994.
—. *The Brotherhood of the Grape*. 1977. Santa Rosa, Ca: Black Sparrow Press, 1990.
—. *Dreams from Bunker Hill*. Santa Rosa, Ca: Black Sparrow Press, 1982.
—. *The Road to Los Angeles*. Santa Rosa, Ca.: Black Sparrow Press, 1985.
—. *Selected Letters 1932-1981*. Santa Rosa, Ca.: Black Sparrow Press, 1991.
—. *Wait Until Spring, Bandini*. 1938. Santa Rosa, Ca: Black Sparrow Press, 1997.
—. *The Wine of Youth: Selected Stories*. 1985. Santa Rosa, Ca: Black Sparrow Press, 1994.
Ford, Hugh. *Published in Paris*. New York: Pushcart Press, 1980.
Gallenga, Antonio. *Episodes of My Second Life*. 2 vols. London: Chapman and Hall, 1884.
Gardaphé, Fred L. "From Oral Tradition to Written Word: Toward an Ethnographically Based Literary Criticism." *From the Margin: Writings in Italian Americana*. Ed. Anthony Julian Tamburry, Paolo A. Giordano, and Fred L. Gardaphe. West Lafayette, In.: Purdue University Press, 1991. 294-306.
—. *Italian Signs, American Streets: The Evolution of Italian American Narrative*. Durham, N. C.: Duke University Press, 1996.
Gelormini, Mario. "Reconstructions of Emanuel Carnevali's *The First God*." Diss. University of Venice "Ca' Foscari," 1992-93.
Gilmore, David D. *Manhood in the Making: Cultural Concepts of Masculinity*. New Haven & London: Yale University Press, 1990.
Hawthorne, Nathaniel. *The Marble Faun: or, The Romance of Monte Beni*. Columbus: Ohio State University Press, 1968.
Herzfeld, Michael. *The Poetics of Manhood: Contest and Identity in a Cretan Mountain Village*. Princeton: Princeton University Press, 1985.
Jakobson, Roman, and Linda R. Waugh. *La forma fonica della lingua*. Trans. Flavia Ravazzoli, Elisabetta Fava, Maria Di Salvo, and Marco Mazzoleni. Milano: Il Saggiatore, 1984.
McFadden, Elizabeth. *The Glitter and the Gold; A Spirited Account of the Metropolitan Museum of Art's First Director, The Audacious and High-Handed Luigi Palma di Cesnola*. New York: The Dial Press, 1971.
Mangione, Jerre. *The Dream and the Deal: The Federal Writers' Project 1935-1943*. Boston: Little, Brown, 1972.
—. *An Ethnic at Large: A Memoir of America in the Thirties and Forties*. New York: G. P. Putnam's Sons, 1978.
—. *Mount Allegro: A Memoir of Italian American Life*. 1943. New York: Harper & Row, 1989.
—. *Reunion in Sicily*. 1950. New York: Columbia University Press, 1984.
—. *The World Around Danilo Dolci; A Passion for Sicilians*. 1968. New York: Harper Colophon Books, 1972.
Marazzi, Martino. *Misteri di Little Italy: Storie e testi della letteratura italoamericana*. Milano: Franco Angeli, 2001.
Marinacci, Barbara. *They Came From Italy; The Stories of Famous Italian-Americans*. New York: Dodd, Mead & Company, 1967.
Martelli, Sebastiano, ed. *Il sogno italo-americano. Realtà e immaginario dell'emigrazione neglitati Uniti*. Napoli: CUEN, 1998.
Maxwell, William. *So Long, See You Tomorrow*. New York: Knopf, 1980.
Murphy, Peter F. Introduction. *Fictions of Masculinity: Crossing Cultures, Crossing Sexualities*. New York & London: New York University Press, 1994. 1-17.
Passarini, Ludovico. *Modi di dire proverbiali e motti popolari italiani*. Roma: Tip. Tiberina, 1875.

Pearce, Roy Harvey. *Savagism and Civilization*. Berkeley: U of California Press, 1988.
Pound, Ezra. "Hugh Selwyn Mauberley." *Selected Poems 1908- 1959*. London: Faber and Faber, 1984. 98-112.
Pynchon, Thomas. *The Crying of Lot 49*. Philadelphia: Lippincott, 1966.
Segale, Sister Blandina. *At the End of the Santa Fe Trail*. 1932. Foreword by Marc Simmons. Albuquerque: University of New Mexico Press, 1999.
Sollors, Werner. *Beyond Ethnicity: Consent and Descent in American Culture*. Oxford: Oxford University Press, 1986.
Tamburri, Anthony Julian, Paolo A. Giordano and Fred L. Guardaphe', ed. *From the Margin: Writings in Italian Americana*. West Lafayette, Indiana: Purdue University Press, 1991.
—. *A Semiotic of Ethnicity: In (Re)Cognition of the Italian American Writer*. New York: State University of New York Press, 1998.
Tanner, Tony. *City of Words: American Fiction 1950-1970*. London: Jonathan Cape, 1971.
Thoreau, Henry D. *Walden*. Ed. J. Lyndon Shanley. Princeton: Princeton University Press, 1971.
Twain, Mark. *Adventures of Huckleberry Finn*. Ed. Walter Blair and Victor Fisher. Berkeley: University of California Press, 1985.
Verdicchio, Pasquale. *Approaches to Absence*. Montreal: Guernica, 1994.
—. *A Critical Geography*. San Diego: Parentheses, 1990. Revised ed. in *Approaches to Absence*. 33-41.
—. *Moving Landscape*. Montreal: Guernica, 1985.
—. *Nomadic Trajectory*. Montreal: Guernica, 1990.
—. *The Posthumous Poet: A Suite for Pier Paolo Pasolini*. Los Angeles: Jahbone Press, 1993.
—. *Devils in Paradise: Writings on Post-Emigrant Cultures*. Toronto: Guernica,1997.
Vittorini, Elio, ed. *Americana. Raccolta di narratori dalle origini ai nostri giorni*. Milano: Bompiani,1941.
Whitman, Walt. "There Was a Child Went Forth." *Leaves of Grass*. Ed. Malcolm Cowley. Harmondsworth: Penguin, 1959. 138-139.
Williams, William Carlos. *The Autobiography of William Carlos Williams*. New York: New Directions, 1967.

Printed in June 2003
at Gauvin Press Ltd.
Hull, Québec, Canada